SHOOTING SPORTS SURVEY

CONSERVATION
AND SPORT

JULIANNE VERSNEL GOTTLIEB
EDITOR

MERRIL PRESS
BELLEVUE, WASHINGTON

Shooting Sports Survey

is published by

Merril Press, P.O. Box 1682, Bellevue, WA 98009

www.merrilpress.com

Phone: 425-454-7008

Distributed to the book trade by

Midpoint Trade Books, 27 W. 20th Street, New York, N.Y. 10011

www.midpointtradebooks.com

Phone: 212-727-0190

FIRST EDITION

LIBRARY OF CONGRESS CATALOGING-IN-PUBLICATION DATA

SHOOTING SPORTS SURVEY : CONSERVATION AND SPORT / EDITED BY JULIANNE VERSNEL GOTTLIEB.
   P. CM.
 ISBN 978-0-936783-54-3
 1. SHOOTING. 2. SHOOTING--SOCIOLOGICAL ASPECTS. I. GOTTLIEB, JULIANNE VERSNEL.
 GV1153.S55 2008
 799.2'028'34--DC22

            2008021401

PRINTED IN THE UNITED STATES OF AMERICA

Table of Contents

INTRODUCTION

Governments around the world are facing a dilemma regarding how best to draw a distinction between illegal trafficking in weapons and the perfectly legitimate private sporting arms. This need not be a daunting task.

Law abiding citizens, by definition, are not the problem. Law-abiding hunters, sport shooter and other legal firearms owners have historically helped governments maintain the peace. Hundreds of millions of sporting and subsistence firearms have traditionally and historically been in the hands of families in free nations all over the world where people have lived in peace and enjoyed the lowest of crime rates.

The current international debate on gun control, however, ignores the necessity of hunting, the broader issue of choice of means for personal defense and the unsavory roots of prohibition based on colonialism, classism and racism.

Some guidance on this question can be drawn from the history of North America, where firearms ownership is commonplace.

The North American experience runs counter to the typical historic model, in which colonial entries by European nations into Asia and especially Africa frequently established rules and laws that disarmed the local population but allowed colonists and the colonial governments to have something of a monopoly on arms, for hunting and community defense. This established a pattern in which small arms possession became a symbol of the elite and the government; hardly the model of modern societies that stress equality among all peoples.

Both he United States and Canada rejected this model early in their histories, recognizing the importance of individual firearm ownership on the frontier, where the gun became a tool for putting meat on the table, fending off predatory animals and the common defense. While this tradition is perhaps unique to North America, nonetheless it has applications for other situations. . In the United States, law-abiding citizens are able to own all sorts of firearms that fall under the definition of "small arms," including rifles, shotguns and handguns, and while there are certain regulations regarding their ownership and use, the tradition of gun ownership runs deep and the nation enjoys a record of declining accidents and crime while at the same time experiencing an increasing rate of gun ownership.

It is important to note that widespread gun ownership has proven to be of essential to the environment. Sport and subsistence hunting has become a cornerstone tool of modern wildlife management, as a growing human population expands into areas previously occupied only by wild animals, with sufficient predation to keep populations of those earlier eras in check.

Today, however, man has discovered that animal populations are remarkably adaptable to a changing social landscape, and where once it might have been considered rare to find species like deer, black bear, moose, elk, mountain lions and coyotes coexisting with human populations in many parts of the United States, this is becoming increasingly commonplace. Elsewhere in the world, as other nations modernize and their populations expand into areas previously wild, this interaction between humans and wildlife is inevitable, and only through sound management practices that must include hunting by citizens who are licensed to do so will there be any hope of maintaining manageable wildlife populations while preventing overpopulation and subsequent declines due to starvation and disease.

The North American model provides general opportunity sport and subsistence hunting at key times of the year, primarily in the autumn, and millions of Americans participate in this annual tradition. The result of this hunting carries with it enormous collateral benefits, including the infusion of millions of dollars into the economy, which is particularly important for wildlife management agencies.

This model has been proven in other nations. Sweden and other Scandinavian nations, hunting for subsistence remains a key element of their management programs.

Similarly, hunting in South America, New Zealand and elsewhere, not to mention South Africa and Zimbabwe, has attracted sportsmen from all over the world. In the African nations, this hunting contributes directly to local subsistence as none of the harvested meat is wasted, nor is it exported.

The United States and European models also includes gun collecting, which is widespread and covers virtually all types of firearms, from virtually every period up to modern times. These collections may be for display only, or they may well be "working guns" that are regularly used for any number of reasons, including hunting, predator control, target shooting and competition. Such collections may involve dozens, even scores of firearms, often of museum quality or otherwise historically valuable.

All of this contrasts with the concerns over trafficking in light weapons that may be used by oppressive governments or rogue organizations. There is no debate concerning the need to control or destroy unwanted stockpiles of small arms, light weapons and ammunition. All legitimate firearms owners, hunters, collectors and sport shooters have a vested interest in the legal transfer of firearms.

As the Organization of American States Firearms Protocol acknowledges, hunters, sportsmen and collectors have certain inherent rights.

> Recognizing that states have developed different cultural and historical uses for firearms, and that the purpose of enhancing international cooperation to eradicate illicit transnational trafficking in firearms is not intended to discourage or diminish lawful leisure or recreational activities such as travel or tourism for sport shooting, hunting, and other forms of lawful ownership and use recognized by the States Parties. (http://www.oas.org/juridico/English/treaties/a-63.html)

With over twenty authors and dozens of organizations in almost forty countries, the Shooting Sports Survey addresses the legitimate, legal and beneficial aspects of individual small arms ownership internationally.

Julianne Versnel Gottlieb

INTERNATIONAL SHOOTING SPORTS

AUSTRALIA

AUSTRALIA'S GUN LAWS SINCE 1996

produced by SSAA Inc* Media & Publications

BACKGROUND AND COMPULSORY BUYBACK

www.ssaa.org.au

In 1996, Australia's gun laws and regulations came to the fore after a mass-shooting incident in Port Arthur, Tasmania, in which 35 people were killed and 37 injured by Martin Bryant with two military-style self-loading rifles. Bryant was a mentally challenged man with a low IQ and had exhibited disturbing behaviour for many years prior. He was ineligible for a firearm licence and had acquired the firearms illegally when he murdered two people with a knife and stole their firearms.

Within a short period of time, newly-elected Prime Minister John Howard pressured the state governments, who control gun laws in Australia, to administer radical, reactionary and sweeping gun laws in the form of the National Firearm Agreement 1996, the crux of which was the compulsory buyback of self-loading longarms. The Federal Government put a 1% increase on the Medicare levy for one year to finance the purchase and destruction of all self-loading rifles including .22 rimfires, self-loading shotguns and pump-action shotguns.

Australia's Matthew Harriman won the Junior Division of the Bianchi International Speed Event at the 2007 NRA Bianchi Cup held at the Green Valley Rifle and Pistol Club's Chapman Academy Range outside Columbia, Missouri.

The buyback was implemented at a reported cost of half a billion dollars. Firearm retailers and wholesalers were compensated for their compulsory loss of stock and some businesses were paid to shut their doors. Mandatory gun licences and registration of all firearms and a near-total ban on all self-loading rifles and shotguns and all pump-action shotguns were the result. Some farmers, professional cullers and sportspeople were permitted to own certain self-loading rifles and shotguns, but the majority of licensed firearm owners, including international sporting shooters, were banned from legally acquiring and owning these firearms for recreational target shooting and hunting. The modus operandi of the buyback was to create a safer community through lower crime and suicide rates and to prevent such a mass-shooting occurring again in Australia.

SSAA promotes the safe handling and storage of firearms at all times.

In 2002, international university student Huan Yun 'Allen' Xiang shot at his classmates and teacher, killing two and injuring five people, at the Monash University in Victoria. Prior to the shooting, members of Xiang's university had expressed concerns about his mental state. During the trial, the defence and prosecution agreed that Xiang suffered from paranoid delusional disorder. Xiang himself argued that he felt the killings were his destiny. In June 2004, the Victorian Supreme Court jury found Xiang not guilty due to mental impairment and he was subsequently sent to a psychiatric hospital. Once again, a man known to have suffered mental illness committed criminal acts.

Prime Minister John Howard's Government again reviewed the gun laws and tightened the control of handguns used for sport shooting and even those held as part of an historical collection. The Federal Government also introduced another firearm buyback. The National Handgun Buyback Act 2003 came into law on June 30, 2003, and brought new restrictions on maximum calibre, magazine capacity and minimum barrel lengths for single-shot firearms, revolvers and self-loaders. Sporting shooters were, and still are to this day, prohibited from importing, purchasing, possessing or using a handgun which has a calibre greater than .38 (the only two exceptions being to participate in SSAA's Single Action or Handgun Metallic Silhouette competitions) and a barrel length less than 120mm for self-loading handguns and 100mm for revolvers and single-shot handguns.

The Federal Government, through the states and territories, also introduced a variety of strict regulations for sporting handgun use. These regulations include undertaking formalised safety training (either through a club framework or external education agency); a probationary period within a club, during which time they are not allowed to purchase a handgun; ongoing safety instruction; a nation-wide personal criminal record check; minimum number of visits per year to a recognised shooting club; waiting periods and police checks when purchasing a firearm and firearm storage regime checks.

Australian Double Trap shooters Craig Trembath and Russell Mark were triumphant at the 2006 Commonwealth Games.

THE FALLOUT

The National Firearms Agreement 1996 and the National Handgun Buyback Act 2003 were, in the words of the Federal Government, introduced to curb firearm violence and make the Australian community safer. Since 1996, firearms violence has indeed dropped and the government and many anti-gun groups attribute this to the new strict firearms regulations and buybacks.

However, further research suggests that firearms violence was actually decreasing prior to the buybacks anyway. According to the Homicide in Australia: 2001-2002 National Homicide Monitoring Program (NHMP) Annual Report, despite an overall increase in homicide victimisation in 2001-02, there was a decrease in the number of recorded homicides where the type of weapon used was a firearm.

Between July 1, 1989, and June 20, 2002, there was a gradual decline in the use of firearms to commit homicide too. Firearms were used in 26 per cent of homicides in Australia in 1989-90, compared to 14 per cent in 2001-02. This represents a 25 per cent decrease and is the lowest proportion of homicides committed with a firearm since the inception of the NHMP in 1990. The most common type of firearms used to commit homicide in 2001-02 were handguns (56 per cent); however, in most cases, the firearm used in the homicide was not registered or licensed to either the victim or the offender.

In 2000, a report by the Australian Institute of Criminology titled 'The Licensing and Registration Status of Firearms Used in Homicide' found that since 1997 licensed firearms owners were not responsible for more than 90% of firearm-related homicides. Indeed, 97% of firearms used in homicides were not registered and almost none of the owners were licensed.

The incidences of suicide committed with a firearm has also dropped. The Institute of Criminology's 2003 report 'Firearm Related Deaths in Australia, 1991-2001' found a 47% decrease in firearm-related death numbers, with a fall in the number of suicides accounting for the largest part of that decrease.

The SSAA's 1999 report, Suicide Update, which contains data from the Bureau of Statistics, found that seven out of Australia's eight states and territories finished the year 1997 with higher standardised death rates from suicide than they had a decade before. There is some evidence, however, to suggest that there has been a gradual decrease in the number of suicides. From the report, it is also evident that the manner in which suicides are carried out has been changing. For instance, where firearms may have been used in the past, methods such as gases, vapours, hanging, strangulation and suffocation are now often used. It is important to also remember that in nations where firearm ownership is heavily restricted, such as Japan, suicide rates continue to be high.

MENTAL HEALTH

According to the Out of Hospital, Out of Mind report by the Mental Health Council, every society will have people who commit suicide…that is a tragic fact of life. However, in order to try and decrease the numbers of people committing suicide, services and education must be available everywhere. The report furthermore states that the personal and social cost of almost two decades of chronic under-funding for mental healthcare is immeasurable. In 2001, 2454 people died by suicide, representing 4.4% of all deaths among people aged less than 75. The vast majority of those committing suicide had

Top photo: Australian Rifle Metallic Silhouette shooters Matthew Everingham and Dann Suthern at the 2006 Inaugural Pacific Regional Championships. Middle photo: An Australian competitor takes aim in the Rifle Metallic Silhouette competition at the 2006 Inaugural Pacific Regional Championships. Bottom photo: New Zealand competitors take to the Field Rifle/3-Positional competition at the 2006 Inaugural Pacific Regional Championships.

untreated mental disorders, particularly depression and alcohol or drug abuse. Many of these could have responded to early intervention treatment, reducing the numbers of mentally-ill people who commit suicide or are incarcerated for criminal acts.

The SSAA, in voice with many international academics and criminologists, have always counselled that money spent on mental health will have far better results on the occurrence of crime than merely restricting gun use to law-abiding citizens. In 2007, the Federal Government allocated $1.8 billion over five years to its decaying mental health services after years of neglect. The results of this funding are yet to be seen, but will be monitored and examined.

Interestingly, the most recent mass murders were committed not with a firearm, but with matches. In 2000, Robert Paul Long killed 15 backpackers at the Childers Palace Backpackers Hostel fire in Queensland. Long was arrested for lighting the fire and charged with two counts of murder and one count of arson. He was a pathological liar who had been previously convicted of burglary and assault and had a known history of leaving fake suicide notes and unexplained fires. Long was subsequently sentenced to life in prison for the Childers fire and murders. He was not known to have used firearms in any of his crimes.

The issue of mentally ill people being housed in backpacker hostels intended as affordable accommodation for international youth tourists (instead of being housed in accredited and recognised mental health residences) and the potential it brings for conflict has also been raised as an issue.

ORGANISED CRIME

One of the recent law and order issues has been the exposure of outlaw motorcycle groups in firearm-related and organised crime. Surprisingly, the media has generally been responsible of its reporting of firearm-related crimes when those crimes are committed by members of gangs and organised crime syndicates.

In 2007, a shooting in Melbourne raised the issue of handgun ownership again. This time, however, the media took a very different stance of the issue of firearms when it became known that the perpetrator was a member of a bikie gang and had obtained his firearms illegally. The extreme anti-gun lobby, of course, raised arguments against civilian firearm ownership, but their arguments were quickly deflated by the seemingly more reasonable and logical arguments from the media. The media continued to report, and appropriately so, that the tragedy had more to do with law and order issues, than the current firearm ownership regulations for law-abiding citizens.

THE FUTURE OF AUSTRALIA'S GUN LAWS

SSAA actively encourages junior shooters and hunters to become members through their 'Sign Up A Junior' campaigns and supports them with many and varied junior-specific shooting programs and activities.

The SSAA, like many other groups from around the world, have expended a lot of time and money in countering both the Federal and State Government and the media's demonising of law-abiding, licensed and legitimate firearm owners. With the change of

Federal Government in late 2007 and the now Prime Minister Kevin Rudd's public acknowledgement of his enjoyment of recreational shooting and his interest in the mechanics of firearms, the opportunity presents itself for a clean slate to promote recreational shooting and hunting in Australia. However, only time will tell.

Despite expenditure of close to three-quarters of a billion dollars, the reality remains that only the unlawful use firearms in the commission of crime. Australia is and has always been a comparatively safe community and the SSAA will continue to educate shooters in the safe, responsible and lawful manner of firearm use. While Australia has had firearms taken away and stricter regulations have been introduced, sport shooting and hunting remains a valid and important pastime in the Australian culture and continues to attract international firearm enthusiasts.

* Sporting Shooters Association of Australia

> SSAA National office
> Postal address: PO Box 762, Kent Town, South Australia 5071 Australia
> Phone number: +61 8 8272 7100
> Email: mh@ssaa.org.au
> Website: www.ssaa.org.au
> Magazine website: www.australianshooter.com.au

References:

Australian Institute of Criminology 2007, 'Criminal Use of Handguns in Australia', Crime and Criminal Justice Statistics, July 2007, http://www.aic.gov.au/stats/crime/keyFacts_handguns.html

Australian Institute of Criminology 2003, 'Decrease in Firearm Homicides', Crime Facts Info, July 22 2003, no. 54, http://www.aic.gov.au/publications/cfi/cfi054.html

Groom, G, Hickie, I & Davenport, T 2003, Out of Hospital, Out of Mind: Review of Mental Health Services in Australia, April 2003, Mental Health Council of Australia, http://www.mhca.org.au/Publications/documents/OutofHospitalOutofMind.pdf

Mouzos, J & Rushforth, C 2003, 'Firearm Related Deaths in Australia, 1991-2001, Trends & Issues in Crime and Criminal Justice, November 2003, no. 269, http://www.aic.gov.au/publications/tandi2/tandi269.pdf

Mouzos, J 2000, 'The Licensing and Registration Status of Firearms Used in Homicide', Trends & Issues in Crime and Criminal Justice, May 2000, no. 151, http://www.aic.gov.au/publications/tandi/tandi151.html

SSAA Inc 2007, Melbourne Shootings, June 21 2007, http://www.ssaa.org.au/newssaa/pressreleases/pr210607.html

SSAA Inc 2006, Handgun Ownership Facts in Australia, http://www.ssaa.org.au/newssaa/noticeboardarchive/handgun-ownership-facts.html

SSAA Inc 2006, Ten Years After the National Firearms Agreement of 1996, http://www.ssaa.org.au/newssaa/noticeboardarchive/ten-years-Firearms-Agreement.html

SSAA Inc 1999, Suicide Update, March 1999, http://www.ssaa.org.au/newssaa/political%20archive/legislativereports/ilamch99.htm

AUSTRIA

THE EU-DIRECTIVE AND SPORT SHOOTING IN AUSTRIA

Franz Császár

In Austria, sport shooting with rifles and shotguns will be severely affected by the coming revised European Union (EU) Arms Directive.

In order to comply with the United Nations Firearms Protocol, the EU had to adapt its original directive of 1991. A small minority of members of the European Parliament took this as a welcome opportunity to call for far-reaching restrictions on civilian arms ownership. There was only weak support for the Austrian position that there is no real need for such a step, as most of the proposed requirements are already enforced in most of the European countries. However, through intense negotiations it was possible to avert some of these new proposals.

Sport shooting has a long established and firmly rooted tradition in Austria. The Sport Shooting Organisation of Austria was founded in 1879. At present it has about 750 clubs with more than 30,000 members. Austrian shooters figure prominently in international competition. Part of this might be attributed to the traditionally very liberal firearms laws, in particular concerning longarms. It will be in this field where the new directive will be felt most severely.

In Austria, the acquisition and possession of single shot and repeating rifles and shotguns have been virtually unrestricted up till now, the only requirements being a minimum age of 18 and the absence of a serious criminal record. For sport shooting this age limit can be lowered to 16 years. For use on commissioned target ranges no age limit applies at all. Since 1996, when the original directive came into effect, rifles, their owners and any change of the ownership of the gun have to be registered with any licensed dealer; shotguns have not had to be registered at all.

This will be a thing of the past. Acquisition and possession of longarms will require a licence based on "good reason". However, shooting sports will be recognised as such. Moreover, a central state registration of all longarms and their owners has to be established, covering all newly acquired arms (either from firearms dealers or from private owners) and in the case of rifles even for all guns already in legal possession (and registered) without any change of owner. In effect the already existing, much stricter regime on handguns will apply to long guns in the future. It is, however, to be hoped that some further requirements relating to handguns (and semi-automatic long guns), such as, for instance a psychological test and rather narrow restrictions on the number of guns allowed, will not come into force.

The Austrian crime situation can by no means serve as an excuse to implement such measures. (There are very good reasons to doubt the efficacy of such an approach at all, as worldwide the overall outcome of stricter guns laws has been an increase in the number of illegal guns and rising gun crime.) Although the number of legal handgun owners has increased 90% between 1982 and 1997 with a following 30% decrease till 2007, from 1998 to 2005 total murder (including attempts) has remained stable at a comparatively low level and total suicide has decreased 30%. From 1998 to 2007, only 5% of all murder cases have been committed with a legal firearm.

The new rules do not offer any realistic advantage in crime prevention or police clearance work. In that connection, it should be mentioned that in 2007 more than 40% of the suspects of murder, attempted murder and serious assaults have been non-Austrians. The crime-prone segment of this part of the population is in general not on record as bothering to comply with the Austrian gun laws.

The registration scheme poses severe challenges in manpower and funds for the police. For legal gun owners all this will bring at best a lot of nuisance and very likely financial expenses.

However, because for some time civilian firearms ownership has ceased to be a political issue between the main political parties, there is a good chance that the EU requirements will be implemented in a reasonable way. The Austrian manufacturers, arms dealers, hunters, sport shooters, collectors and other private arms owners have for the first time explicitly taken a common stance. There exists a positive working relation with the Ministry of Interior, in charge of drafting the new rules. All this will be of paramount importance not only for the new law in itself but also for its fair administration.

CANADA

AN EVALUATION OF THE CANADIAN FIREARMS REGISTRY

Gary Mauser

In 1995, the Canadian government passed legislation that would institute universal firearms registration. This legislation assumed that, by controlling the availability of firearms, the firearms registry would reduce total criminal violence. At the time the legislation was introduced, the federal government claimed that requiring hunters and target shooters to get a firearms licence and register their firearms would reduce rates of total homicide, criminal violence, and domestic violence. But public safety improved since Canada made universal firearms registration mandatory in 1998. Let us examine the data.

The vast majority of Canadians who own firearms do so for legal purposes. Approximately three-quarters of owners say that they have firearms primarily for hunting. Another 13% answer they are target shooters; smaller percentages give other reasons, e.g., pest control, self protection, or collection. Canadian hunters are vitally important for wildlife conservation. They pay governments almost $70 million annually for hunting permits and voluntarily contribute an additional $33 million for conservation protects. In total, hunters contribute an estimated $10 billion to the Canadian economy. Hunters also are important in controlling wildlife populations.

The first question is the most fundamental: has there been a decline in firearms availability since the introduction of the firearms registry? The answer is clear: the number of firearm owners has declined

Women's Handgun training class

substantially. The best estimate is that there were between 4.5 and 5.5 million firearm owners prior to the 1995 legislation. Some reputable estimates are even higher. By 1996, this number had dropped to between 3.5 and 4 million firearms owners (Mauser, 2001; Mauser and Buckner, 1997). After firearms registration was introduced in 1998, it dropped still further. I estimate there were between 3 and 3.5 million firearm owners in Canada by 2002 (Mauser, 2007). There were probably fewer still in 2008, although it is likely that the rate of decline has slowed.

The next question is whether licensing and registration have improved public safety. Specifically, can it be shown to have reduced homicide, criminal violence, and domestic violence?

Homicide. Since the firearms registry was introduced in 1998, the Canadian homicide rate has remained stable [figure 1]. According to the most recent statistics for 2006, the homicide rate is the same as it was in 1998 (Li, 2007). This trend offers no support for the argument that the registry has improved public safety. The homicide rate had been declining before the registry was introduced.

An inspection of the Canadian homicide data shows that the percentage of homicides involving a firearm over the past decade has been basically stable. The percentage of homicides involving firearms was 31% in 1993, 34% in 2005, and 31% in 2006 (Dauvergne and De Socio, 2007). The stability in homicides involving firearms suggests that homicide rates are driven by factors such as demographics or economics, not by a change in the lawful availability of firearms (Bunge, 2005; Kates and Mauser, 2007). Again, this does not lend support to the claim that the firearms registry has been effective.

In contrast, the number of homicides that are related to gang activity has increased since the early 1990s, and since 1998 [figure 1]. Gang-related murders typically involve handguns. Although handguns have been registered since the 1930s, this has not reduced the level of their criminal misuse. Studies have consistently shown that the vast bulk of guns used in crime are smuggled (Breitkreuz, 2006).

Violent crime. The rate of violent crime has decreased by 3% since the firearms registry was introduced in 1998 (Silver, 2007). However, it is difficult to credit the gun registry for the decline because it started considerably before firearms registration was introduced. As well, since handguns play a bigger role in criminal violence than do long guns, and the primary focus of the firearms registry is on long guns, the registry would not be expected to have a significant impact on criminal violence involving handguns.

As prominent criminologists have predicted, the firearms registry has not had a significant impact on criminal violence (Gabor, 1995). Since few of the firearms used by criminals are registered, or have ever been registered, firearm regulations have little effect on their access to firearms. To the extent that firearm registration does limit criminal access to firearms, these restrictions merely increases the cost of illegal firearms. More serious criminals appear willing to pay the higher prices for firearms while less serious criminals substitute other weapons in order to commit violent crimes.

Target shooting

Domestic violence. Contrary to the government's claims in 1995, the firearms registry did not have an observable impact on domestic violence. An analysis of the 2004 General Social Survey (GSS) shows that the percentage (7%) of Canadians 15 years of age and older who reported that they had experienced spousal violence over the previous 5 years has not changed since the previous GSS in 1999 (Milhorean, 2005).

In conclusion, my analysis suggests that licensing and registration very likely contributed to the shrinking numbers of firearm owners but there is no evidence to suggest that they have influenced gun violence, including homicides involving firearms. Nor was the firearm registry associated with a drop in either the overall homicide rate or the violent crime rate. This conclusion is consistent with other research (Bunge et al., 2005; Kleck, 1997: 377). Powerful econometric studies could not find an impact of earlier Canadian gun laws on either homicide (Mauser and Holmes, 1992) or violent crime (Mauser and Maki, 2003). Murder appears to depend primarily upon motive, not the availability of a particular tool. Unfortunately, many deadly alternatives exist to firearms. Contrary to the purported findings of case-control studies, homicides are not more likely to occur in homes with firearms. No support was found in these econometric studies for the claim that Canadian gun laws have saved any lives by reducing homicide. Future analyses, when more data become available, may of course modify these conclusions.

REFERENCES

Breitkreuz, Garry. Media release. "5,194 homicides in 9 years: Only 2.27% of guns were registered," December 7, 2006. http://www.garrybreitkreuz.com/breitkreuzgpress/2006/dec7.htm

Bunge, Valerie Pottie, Holly Johnson, and Thierno Baldé (2005). Exploring Crime Patterns in Canada. Crime and Justice Research Paper Series. Statistics Canada.

Dauvergne, Mia (2005). Homicide in Canada, 2004. Juristat 25, 6. Statistics Canada.

Dauvergne, Mia and Leonardo De Socio (2007). "Firearms and Violent Crime," Juristat, Vol 28, No 2, Statistics Canada.

Federal Bureau of Investigation [FBI] (2006). Crime in the United States 2005. Uniform Crime Reporting Program (September 18). <http://www.fbi.gov/ucr/05cius/>.

Gabor, Thomas (1995). The Proposed Canadian Legislation on Firearms: More Symbolism than Prevention. Canadian Journal of Criminology 37, 2 (April): 195–219.

Kates, Don B., and Gary Mauser (2007). Would Banning Firearms Reduce Murder and Suicide? A Review of International Evidence. Harvard Journal of Law and Public Policy 30, 2 (Spring): 649–94.

Kleck, Gary (1997). Targeting Guns: Firearms and Their Control. Aldine de Gruyter.

Li, Geoffrey (2007). "Homicide in Canada, 2006," Juristat, Vol 27, No 8, Statistics Canada.
Mauser, Gary (2001). Misfire: Firearm Registration in Canada. Public Policy Sources 48. The Fraser Institute.

Mauser, Gary (2007). Hubris in the North: The Canadian Firearms Registry. Originally an invited keynote presentation at: In the Right Hands – an international firearm safety seminar, held in Christchurch, New Zealand, 21-23 February 2006. Public Policy Sources, The Fraser Institute, Vancouver BC.

Mauser, Gary (2008). "Firearms," in Prohibitions, John Meadowcroft (ed.), The Institute of Economic Affairs, London, England.

Mauser, Gary, and Taylor Buckner (1997). Canadian Attitudes toward Gun Control: The Real Story. The Mackenzie Institute.

Mauser, Gary and Richard Holmes (1992). "An evaluation of the 1977 Canadian Firearms Legislation," Evaluation Review, Vol. 16, No 6, pp 603-617.

Mauser, Gary and Dennis Maki. "An Evaluation of the 1977 Canadian Firearms Legislation: Robbery Involving a Firearm." Applied Economics, Vol. 35, March 2003, 423-436.

Milhorean, Karen (2005). Trends in Self Reported Spousal Violence. In Kathy AuCoin, ed., Family Violence in Canada: A Statistical Profile 2005 (Statistics Canada): 13–32.

Silver, Warren (2007). "Crime Statistics in Canada, 2006," Juristat, Vol 27, No 5, Statistics Canada.

BRITAIN

SHOOTING IN BRITAIN

By David Penn, Secretary, British Shooting Sports Council*

HISTORICAL PERSPECTIVE

Back in 1979, a journalist called Edward Baxter termed shooting 'The Invisible Sport', flourishing, but unnoticed.

It was not always so. By the middle of the 19th Century shooting as a sport was spreading widely among the middle classes, and was a high-profile activity encouraged by the Royal Family and many influential individuals. Competitive rifle shooting grew out of the Volunteer Rifle movement of the 1860s, born of a fear of French invasion and reaching 171,000 civilian riflemen by 1861, which began a close relationship between target rifle shooting and the military that still endures. The National Rifle Association was founded in November 1859, 12 years ahead of its American counterpart, and target shooting was treated by the media as a mainstream sport, with 80 reporters covering the NRA's 1905 meeting at Bisley Camp and writing over a million words of text. The first reference to competitive (live) pigeon shooting in England was in 1777, and this sport was highly evolved by the 1860s, becoming the precursor of today's clay target shooting. Game shooting was also becoming more accessible to those with disposable incomes, and deer stalking and shooting in Scotland were popularised by Prince Albert, the Prince Consort. By the turn of the century, the growing popularity of 'miniature' rifles (small bore rifles for short range target shooting) and air rifles were providing affordable urban sport for the less well off, with the founding of the Society of Working Men's Rifle Clubs in 1901, to be succeeded by the National Small Bore Rifle Association in 1948. Civilian target shooting was promoted by the Government (in 1900 the Prime Minister Lord Salisbury stated that his intention was that 'a rifle should be kept in every cottage in the land') and the military.

British Shooting Sports Council

This was also the period when Britain, with almost no restrictive firearms legislation, was a major innovator in the field of firearms, with the development of the sporting double barrelled shotgun, cartridges and rifles for dangerous game hunting, double action service revolvers and military rifle cartridges designed for exceptional performance at very long range (both as a defence against field artillery and for the British passion for shooting at targets 1,200 or more yards distant). Revolver shooting as a sport had also seen great development in England.

So how did shooting transmogrify from a high-profile Establishment-encouraged activity into Edward Baxter's 'Invisible Sport' of thirty years ago? During the First World War, the scope and effectiveness of the Government's ability to regulate its citizens' lives increased exponentially, and the first effective firearms controls were introduced to ensure that service calibre small arms were destined solely for the war effort. In the aftermath of conflict, there was a hope that the horrors of war had been consigned to history and a desire to turn away from military matters. With the Firearms Act 1920, there was the first serious attempt to control rifles and pistols in civilian hands, engendered by a desire to control surplus military arms with which Europe was awash, to hinder the acquisition of firearms by Bolshevik revolutionaries and, ostensibly, as an anti-crime measure in the age of the armed 'motor bandit'. Target rifle and pistol shooting entered a quiescent period and faded from public awareness, but retained its military links. In some ways, target shooters felt protected: as early as the 1920 Firearms Act, the concept of the Home Office Approved rifle club came into being, and rifle clubs could benefit financially through becoming charities by virtue of a provision covering activities which contributed to the defence of the realm.

Young shot with gamekeeper. Photograph courtesy Graham Downing. Note the keeper's .22 rifle is fitted with a sound moderator.

Clay pigeon shooting, however, expanded hugely in the 1920s, with the founding of the Clay Pigeon Shooting Association in 1928, with added cachet deriving from the interest of HRH Edward, Prince of Wales. In 1925 the first 'Sporting Clay' competition was inaugurated, introducing what is arguably Britain's greatest contribution to the sport, and one that is increasingly popular today, nationally and internationally.

During the Second World War, rifle clubs provided training facilities and instructors for the armed forces, with a Small Arms School at Bisley, and with many clubs forming the basis of Home Guard units. Post 1945, target shooting continued to operate below the radar, but by the 1960s with a growing interest in more technically sophisticated rifles, rather that the converted service rifles of old, and in pistol shooting, a sport well suited to indoor urban ranges. By the mid-1980s, Britain was host to the world's biggest annual pistol shooting event run by the National Pistol Association.

MODERN LEGISLATION

This tranquil period was ended by a series of event-driven changes in the law. The 1965 Firearms Act required the registration for the first time of dealers in shotguns, and increased the minimum length of a shotgun barrel from 20 to 24 inches. This legislation was passed just before an Act to abolish capital punishment. In August 1966 three police officers were shot dead by petty criminals armed with illegally owned pistols. Strong public revulsion and demands for the re-instatement of the death penalty were countered by the introduction of a licensing system for shotgun owners in the Criminal Justice Act 1967. The British Shooting Sports Council (BSSC) was created from an *ad hoc* committee of all the major target shooting, field sports and gun trade associations that came together in (and was at first named after) Purdey's famous Long Room to operate co-operatively in opposing 1960s legislation.

Its role continues to be to co-ordinate activity on the political and legislative fronts.

In 1973, the Government issued a discussion document on the control of firearms, proposing draconian new controls on firearms, including licensing shotguns in the same way as rifles, a ban on repeating shotguns, on imitation firearms and on collecting. The BSSC led the campaign to protect the sport, while the Ad Hoc Committee on Historic Firearms brought together museums, collectors, the antique arms trade and other heritage interests. The BSSC's and Ad Hoc Committee's opposition was successful, as the proposals were perceived as disproportionate, and they had been introduced when there was no specific public or media concern over firearms.

An 'amok' mass killing in Hungerford in 1987, involving a legally owned AK47-type self-loading rifle, resulted in the banning of semi-automatic and pump action centrefire rifles and some repeating shotguns, and tighter controls on repeating shotguns. After the Dunblane tragedy in 1996, in which a 9mm pistol was used, on a tide of media and public emotion at the time of a general election 'small firearms' (i.e. with a barrel of less than 30cm in length, or an overall length of less than 60cm) were banned for the purpose of target shooting.

SHOOTING SPORTS ORGANISATIONS

Despite these bans, shooters and shooting organisations in Britain have demonstrated considerable resilience and have worked hard not only to strengthen and develop their sport but to improve understanding of their activities among politicians, the police, the media and the public. No longer is it acceptable to be an invisible sport, and the larger organisations have proved increasingly adept at positive public relations.

Quarry shooting has long been safeguarded and publicised by Britain's largest shooting organisation, the British Association for Shooting & Conservation (BASC), which had its beginnings in 1908, with the founding of the Wildfowlers Association of Great Britain and Ireland. In 1981 this became BASC, embracing all forms of quarry shooting, and it is now Britain's largest shooting association, with an all-time high in 2008 of 127,000 members and 100 staff, and a reputation for active protection of its members' interests.

Although its interests are much wider than field sports alone, the Countryside Alliance, founded in 1997 and with 407,000 members has proved not only one of the strongest supporters of shooting and other field sports, but also one of its most effective advocates in the media, for instance through its 'Game to Eat' campaign which has boosted the appreciation of the healthy virtues of game meat among the population at large.

The BSSC has worked on the Churchillian principle that 'jaw, jaw is better than war, war', and events have confirmed that negotiation is

Happy crowds at the Midland Game Fair. Photograph courtesy of the British Association for Shooting and Conservation.

more productive than confrontation. The BSSC is in constant contact with the Home Office, holds regular meetings with the police Firearms & Explosives Licensing Working Group. By ensuring better understanding by the authorities of both the likely real impact of legislative proposals and championing the wishes and expectations of firearms owners, the BSSC has successfully improved or at least considerably mitigated the effects on the law-abiding of legislation which is usually event-driven and intended to combat crime. To raise the profile of the sport among the population at large it holds 'National Shooting Weeks' to encourage people to come along and try target shooting. Game Fairs and Country Fairs also provide an enjoyable introduction to the sport. Acutely aware of the impact of United Nations legislation and of European Union Directives on British shooters and gun owners, the BSSC is a very active member of the World Forum on the Future of Sport Shooting Activities (WFSA).

The interests of those who collect firearms are the concern of the Historical Breechloading Smallarms Association which works closely with the Foundation for European Societies of Arms Collectors (FESAC) and with other national collecting bodies such as the Arms & Armour Society and the Muzzle Loaders Association of Great Britain.

Shooting in Britain attracts girls as well as boys. Photograph courtesy of British Association for Shooting and Conservation.

The legitimacy of shooting as a leisure activity and an essential component of wildlife management is becoming increasingly recognised. The Labour Party's 2005 'Charter for Shooting' endorses self-regulation and recognises that there is no connection between legitimate sporting shooting and gun crime. The Olympic Games have provided an outstanding opportunity for publicity, and the benefits of the shooting sports have been acknowledged by the three major UK political parties.

So let us take an overview of shooting in Britain today:

PARTICIPATION IN THE SHOOTING SPORTS

An estimated one million people in the UK shoot. The number of shotgun certificates is again increasing, as is the number of young people entering the sport. 1,200 entered BASC's Young Shots scheme in just six months in 2007, while the Scout Association's annual rifle competition grows year on year and there is a renaissance of interest in target shooting as a sport in schools.

- Hunting with firearms is a £1.6 billion industry in the United Kingdom, supporting 70,000 jobs, according to the 2006 PACEC** Report. Shooting providers spend an estimated £250 million a year on habitat and wildlife management, five times the annual income of Britain's biggest conservation organisation, the Royal Society for the Protection of Birds.

- 480,000 people shoot game, wildfowl, pigeon and rabbits, accounting for just under 19 million head of game in 2004.

- Britain's deer population continues to increase, as does recreational deer stalking, which is now a well-accepted contributor to deer management. After close co-operation between government and the shooting organizations, the Deer Act has recently been amended to remove anomalies and improve deer welfare.

- 150,000 people shoot clay targets on a regular basis. 'Corporate days' for clay pigeon shooting are also very popular in the business world, and provide an excellent introduction to the sport.

- 250,000 people regularly enjoy target shooting with rifles, muzzle loading pistols and air weapons.

- There are 1,000 shooting clubs in the UK.

- 23 of the UK's 116 medals in the 2006 Commonwealth Games were for shooting, the second highest medal-winning discipline for UK athletes, exceeded only by swimming with 24. England's most decorated Commonwealth medal winner is Mick Gault, with 15 medals. In 2008 he was awarded the Order of the British Empire for his contribution to shooting-with a pistol.

- 'Field target' air rifle was born in Britain and combines high technology, precision marksmanship, range estimation skills and the challenge of varying courses of fire over different distances, so its popularity is easy to understand. It has revolutionized air rifle and pellet design and performance.

- 'F Class'*** centre-fire target rifle shooting is proving popular with a younger age group used to 'high tech' precision equipment in other aspects of their lives.

- Courses of fire for pistols have been adapted for rimfire or lever action centre-fire 'gallery' rifles.

- The British are well aware of their firearms heritage, and the study of firearms, particularly the 'working' firearms of the soldier or hunter, rather than the decorative *arme de luxe,* has involved shooting to determine performance. From this study has grown the very popular sport of 'Classic' shooting, using the arms of the 1850s to 1945 in courses of fire appropriate to their age.

Air Arms EV2 MkII field target air rifle. Photograph courtesy of Air Arms (NSP Engineering Ltd) and the Gun Trade Association.

- Agreement in principle has been reached with the governments in England & Wales and in Scotland for the training of elite pistol shooter in Britain for the 2012 London Olympics.

- Modern Pentathlon for Juniors has introduced young people to air pistol shooting, and forms an important part of the performance pyramid for the National Pistol Squad.

- British shooters seem to shoot far more than their counterparts in other countries. They consume c. 250,000,000 shotgun cartridges a year.

Britain has a proud and continuing shooting and arms collecting heritage, but our shooting organizations have learned that to flourish unseen is not enough. Our task is to achieve an understanding and recognition of our sport among the population at large, and by the politicians and media. Only through knowledge can we finally be rid of the stigmatization and marginalization of the past.

* British Shooting Sports Council
PO Box 53608
London
SE24 9YN
Telephone: 020 7095 8181
www.bssc.org.uk

** 'PACEC' stands for 'Public & Corporate Economic Consultants', a Cambridge-based company which has done much work for Government Departments connected with rural affairs. Its study was carried out at the behest of BASC, the Countryside Alliance, the Country Land and Business Association and the Game Conservancy Trust. It was carried out to a rigorous academic standard and peer group reviewed, so is considered authoritative.

*** 'F Class' is for any rifle firing any cartridge of up to 8mm. Maximum weight 10Kg. Bipod or front rest and sandbag rear rest allowed. Any sights. Any safe trigger weight. Shot prone or supine. All shots gauged with a 7.62mm gauge, regardless of caliber. In practice it is shot in two classes, one using 'as issued' 5.56mm NATO or 7.62mm NATO ammunition, one for anything else. It is shot from 200-1,000 yards.

The member organization of the British Shooting Sports Council are:

- ASSOCIATION OF PROFESSIONAL CLAY TARGET SHOOTING GROUNDS
- ASSOCIATION OF PROFESSIONAL SHOOTING INSTRUCTORS
- BRITISH ASSOCIATION FOR SHOOTING AND CONSERVATION
- COUNTRYSIDE ALLIANCE
- CLAY PIGEON SHOOTING ASSOCIATION
- GUN TRADE ASSOCIATION
- INSTITUTE OF CLAY SHOOTING INSTRUCTORS
- MUZZLE LOADERS ASSOCIATION OF GREAT BRITAIN
- NATIONAL RIFLE ASSOCIATION
- NATIONAL SMALLBORE RIFLE ASSOCIATION
- SPORTSMAN'S ASSOCIATION OF GREAT BRITAIN & NORTHERN IRELAND
- UNITED KINGDOM PRACTICAL SHOOTING ASSOCIATION

MALTA

MALTA'S NEW ARMS ACT

Stephen A. Petroni

The Mediterranean country of Malta has a new and sensible arms law, thanks to an intrepid group of enthusiasts. The new Arms Act 2005 and the corresponding Arms Licensing Regulations 2006 (LN177) came into effect on August 15, 2006, repealing the old Arms Ordinance of 1931. Several years of intensive negotiations between the authorities and the Association of Maltese Arms Collectors & Shooters (AMACS) are finally beginning to bear fruit.

The Republic of Malta has a population of 400,000 living on three islands forming an archipelago in the central Mediterranean with a total area of 121 square miles. It is the smallest member of the European Union, which it joined on May 1st, 2004.

Clay Shooting Range at Bidnija, Malta

The Maltese islands have an extremely colourful history. They have been inhabited since around 5000 BC and the earliest civilisation to take root there built structures which predate the pyramids of Giza by a millennium. Malta's strategic location and its incredible natural harbour drew the powers that held sway over the Mediterranean Sea; the Phoenicians, Carthaginians, Romans, Byzantines, Arabs, Normans, Angevines, Hohenstaufens, Aragonese, Knights Hospitallers, French and finally the British controlled the islands in that order until the Maltese gained Independence on September 21st, 1964.

The presence of so many different peoples and cultures and particularly of their naval and military forces left an indelible mark on the Maltese and their unique language and culture. Moreover, each successive power left a wealth of artifacts that are found in the national museums and in private collections. Arms which were used by the garrison and those which were captured from invading or attacking forces (particularly during the Ottoman Siege of 1655 and the Axis aerial attacks of 1940-1943) enrich the country's historical heritage.

It comes as no surprise therefore that the Maltese are keen collectors of arms and militaria. Moreover, the Maltese excel in shooting sports which until recently were heavily restricted. Possession of firearms was regulated by the Arms Ordinance of 1931 - enacted when Malta was still a British Colony. It gave the Commissioner of Police full discretionary powers. While nothing was banned under the Arms Ordinance, it gave the Police wide discretionary powers and they effectively banned most types of guns. Importation of guns was limited to shotguns before 1996 (some improvements were introduced in September 1995) and later additionally airguns, muzzle loaders and pre-1940 guns.

THE ARMS ACT, 2005 AND THE ARMS LICENSING REGULATIONS, 2006

The old Arms Ordinance of 1931 was repealed and replaced with a new law that introduces significant changes which place Malta in a leading position among EU countries with regard to arms legislation. The Act faithfully transposes the recently amended EU Arms Directive 91/477/EEC into national law, granting enthusiasts full opportunities in their sport and hobby against a background of sensible control. The Act defines various categories of arms and the activities for which they may be kept and/or used. The Commissioner of Police then licenses persons who qualify to participate in such activities and are therefore permitted to acquire and keep the corresponding type of firearms.

Malta MASC FT National 2008

The accent is on the licence holder rather than on the firearm. The rational behind this is that there are no public safety and security issues if firearms are only kept and used by properly-vetted persons. Moreover, the mandatory membership and endorsement of a club guarantees a better understanding of a person's motives for firearms ownership and use.

The Act empowers the Minister responsible for Home Affairs to appoint a "Weapons Board" composed of a maximum of nine members. The posts have so far been allocated as follows: three from the Police and one from the Army representing the official side and four persons from the NGO's which have an interest in collecting, target shooting, skeet & trap shooting and hunting. The Chairman is nominated by the Minister and is usually a retired civil servant. The Board advises the Commissioner of Police with regard to the issue of licences. It is also empowered to make its recommendations to the Minister for further regulation under the Act.

At the very basis of the Act is the classification of arms under three main Schedules:

> **Schedule I** covers fully automatic firearms and other weapons of military use as well as the ammunition for such arms. Although these are prohibited, licensed collectors may acquire and keep them provided that the weapons are approved by Weapons Board as being of pre-1946 manufacture.

> **Schedule II** covers most firearms that have a sporting use such as pistols, rifles, shotguns, airguns, muzzle-loading revolvers and their ammunition as well as crossbows. All these are subject to a Collector Licence (to acquire and keep for collection purposes only) and/or a Target Shooter Licence (to acquire, keep and use on a licensed range).

Schedule III lists all firearms manufactured prior to 1900, replicas of single shot muzzle loaders, deactivated firearms, non-firing imitation guns and edged weapons. These are exempt from any licence or permit but are subject to a declaration.

Applications for the above are submitted to the Police who compile their report and then refer to the Weapons Board which vets shooters' applications (in the case of Collector Licence A an interview is held with the applicant). The WB notifies the Commissioner of Police of its recommendation and the licence is finally issued or refused by the Police. The whole process is legally limited to two

THE COLLECTOR LICENCE

The Arms Act introduces two new Licences which did not exist under the Ordinance. The first of these is the Collector Licence. The Regulations establish two classes of Collector Licences termed "A" and "B". Collector Licence A is aimed at active collectors who are either starting from scratch or who intend to continue building their collections. Collector Licence B may be considered as an ad hoc licence issued in specific cases as explained later.

A WWII German Haenel MP41

Collector Licence A

Members of a recognised organisation for arms collectors are eligible to apply for this licence. Once approved they will be able to acquire and keep any number of firearms (and ammunition) from all three Schedules provided that they manufactured before 1946 or are considered to be rare, artistic or historical. Additionally they may acquire and keep up to ten Schedule II handguns and rifles which are of post-1945 manufacture as well as any number of shotguns, muzzleloaders and airguns.

Collector Licence B

This licence is issued to persons who after the coming into effect of the Arms Act already held firearms licensed under the old Arms Ordinance for collection purposes only. It is also issued to persons who come into possession of firearms by way of inheritance and wish to keep them for collection purposes but have no intention to enlarge the collection.

It is important to note that all firearms manufactured prior to 1900, replicas of single shot muzzle loaders, deactivated firearms, non-firing imitation guns and edged weapons are now listed under Schedule III and are exempt from any form of licence or permit.

THE TARGET SHOOTER LICENCE

Schedule II lists firearms that are permitted for sports shooting, although some items in Schedule III may also be used for such purposes. Enthusiasts may apply for either a Target Shooting licence A or a Target Shooter Licence B or both. The process to obtain a licence consists of a three-tier vetting system: club vetting, Weapons Board and the Police. The Act also provides for the participation of suitably authorised minors in target shooting sports under supervision only. They will not be allowed to acquire and keep a firearm.

Target Shooter Licence A

The Target Shooter Licence A is a totally new licence category that allows both the keeping and use (for target shooting sport only) firearm types previously prohibited under the repealed Arms Ordinance. A person who intends to pursue the sport of target shooting must first sign up with a licensed shooting club and obtain a club recommendation after having attended a firearms handling and safety course.

The Target Shooter Licence A allows the acquisition, keeping and shooting of a maximum of 10 cartridge firearms with rifled barrels i.e. handguns and rifles. 5000 rounds of ammunition may also be kept. Firearms to be used for target shooting are listed on the Target Shooter Licence A document. They must be stored in a gun safe or strong room (the latter in case one also owns a collection under a Collector Licence).

Target Shooter Licence B

The Target Shooter B Licence caters for target shooting with firearms already allowed under the old Arms Ordinance – Shotgun, airguns and muzzle loaders which are now listed under Schedule II and Schedule III. This licence follows a similar procedure as for Target Shooter A licence. However, besides totally new applicants, it is issued for Target Shooters already licensed under the old Arms Ordinance to carry and use firearms that where already available for target shooting before the new Arms Act came into force - meaning shotguns, airguns and muzzle loading firearms. The licence is also issued without the need for additional formality to persons who are in possession of a valid hunting licence and who wish to practice clay pigeon target shooting only. The obligations of the Target Shooter B licence are the same as for Target Shooter Licence A.

A License may be obtained at age 18. However minors may still practice shooting under supervision but not own a firearm. The parents' or legal guardians' consent in required. Additionally there are separate licenses for clubs which may recommend members for collector or target shooter licenses, range operators, dealers and gunsmiths.

THE SIGNIFICANCE OF THE NEW LAW

This new law should be considered in the light of arms legislation in other EU countries which do not have the safety net of a "2nd Amendment" embedded in their constitutions. EU states' gun laws still vary widely in spite of the EU Arms Directive of 1991 which sought to harmonise such legislation.

The recently-amended Directive specifically excludes Collectors from its provisions and allows sufficient room for the practice of sports shooting.

The new Maltese law comes through as a refreshing example of what can be achieved when politicians listen to persons who are fully conversant with the subject, instead of yielding to pressure from groups driven by emotion rather than reason. Malta's Deputy Prime Minister and Minister for Home Affairs described the exercise as a unique example of collaboration between all parties concerned which finally produced a refined and sensible law. Both sides of the House of Representatives were consulted prior to its enactment and their support was unanimous.

COLLECTOR & SHOOTER ORGANISATIONS IN MALTA.

There are several collecting and sports shooting organisations which are active in Malta. These include the Association of Maltese Asrms Collectors & Shooters, the Malta Sports Shooting Federation (MSSF) and the Association of Arms Collectors & Target Shooters (AACTS). Each organisation has its own clubs or sections which practice sports shooting disciplines according to the rules of the international bodies which they are affiliated with. The Malta Arms & Militaria Society represents almost all licensed collectors. It is affiliated with FESAC.

SPORTS SHOOTING

Target Shooting is currently practiced on Army ranges. However the Weapons Board is in the process of vetting applications for at least three pistol/rifle ranges. Additionally there are several Skeet & trap ranges, some of which have been in operation for many decades.

There exists a long hunting tradition in Malta with over 5% of population participating. It is restricted to birds and wild rabbit since there is no big game on the island. Hunting is regulated under the Code of Police Laws (Chapter 9) as well through the Hunting Licences Regulations (LN 145 of 1993). The processing of licenses is via the hunting organisations and tests are carried out by the authority responsible for the environment. Licences are issued by the Police.

NEW ZEALAND

THE NEW ZEALAND ARMS CONTROL REGIME

Inspector Joe Green[1]

INTRODUCTION

New Zealand Firearms License

This paper provides an overview of the New Zealand arms control regime[2]. The writing of this paper is motivated both by a desire to share with others the strengths of that regime, and, following from this, to address what appears to be misunderstandings arising from the much publicised perspective of a very small group of commentators who hold a particular view on arms control[3]. The New Zealand regime is placed within an international context.

THE NEW ZEALAND ARMS CONTROL REGIME

Firearms in New Zealand are primarily controlled by the Arms Act 1983; Arms Regulations 1992 and the Arms (Restricted Weapons and Specially Dangerous Airguns) Order 1984 (see www.legislation. govt.nz). These are expanded by policy directions collated in the New Zealand Arms Manual 2002. These documents need to be read together for a more complete understanding of the New Zealand arms control regime (see www.police.govt.nz/service/firearms).

Central to the New Zealand arms control regime is the licensing of individuals as fit and proper to possess firearms. Those who wish to possess pistols, restricted weapons or military style semi automatic firearms (MSSAs) may apply for an endorsement on their firearms licence. In order to have the endorsement granted they must demonstrate that they are both fit and proper and have cause to possess that firearm4. The issuing of any such endorsement is subject to the direction of the Commissioner[5].

Pistols, restricted weapons and MSSAs may only be sold or supplied to a person holding a permit to procure issued by a member of Police. Individuals are required to confirm having taken possession of these firearms where such a permit has been issued. Police use information from the permit to procure process to record the details of the pistol, restricted weapon or MSSA against the person's firearms licence[6].

Firearms licenses and endorsements are renewable ten yearly on application. This application is for a <u>new licence</u>, with full vetting and security inspection being a requirement. In short, in order to be issued a new licence the applicant must demonstrate that they continue to be fit and proper to possess firearms.

Individuals applying for a firearms licence are determined as being, or not being fit and proper by a vetting process that includes but is not limited to:

1. Information held on Police computer systems, including criminal records, intelligence data and Court Orders such as Family Violence Protection Orders.
2. Face to face interview with the applicant's partner, spouse or next of kin (for both first time applicants and applicants to renew).
3. For first time applicants, face to face interview with an unrelated referee. For renewals this interview may be carried out by telephone.
4. Face to face interview with the applicant.
5. Physical inspection of security in place for firearms. Security requirements are set by regulation.
6. The recording of information about firearms held, ensuring that the security inspected is commensurate with the firearms the applicant claims to possess[7].

Any other inquiry that the Arms Officer considers necessary. This may include obtaining a doctor's certificate.

Those wishing to have an endorsement must further satisfy Police as to their fit and proper status and the reason they wish to possess a pistol, restricted weapon or MSSA.

This process includes:

1. Evidence of bona fide interest in possessing that pistol, restricted weapon or MSSA, that is, meeting the statutory 'cause to possess' required by the Arms Act.
2. Interview of referees who already possess pistols, restricted weapons or MSSAs.
3. For target pistol shooting; confirmation as being the member of a pistol shooting club recognised by the Commissioner of Police.
4. Security commensurate with the type of firearm to be possessed. Security standards for pistols, restricted weapons and MSSAs are of a higher standard than for sporting long arms and are set by regulation.
5. On renewal of the licence/endorsement, a physical audit of pistols, restricted weapons and MSSAs recorded against the applicant's licence
6. Any other inquiry the Arms Officer considers necessary.

Handling firearms safely

Safety information provided by NZ police

Arms Officers are directed in the vetting process by the Vetting Guide and the Vetting Master Guide.

Those wishing to sell or manufacture firearms by way of business are required to apply to Police for a dealers licence. The arms dealers licence is issued on the basis that a person demonstrates that they are fit and proper to carry out this business. Dealers and their employees are also required to hold a firearms licence, and if selling pistols, restricted weapons or MSSAs the requisite endorsement. Security and recording requirements for Dealers are set by Regulation. The Dealer's licence is renewable annually.

ACTIONS OF FIT AND PROPER PERSONS

Having been determined as fit and proper to use, possess or sell and manufacture firearms indicates that an individual is likely to possess and use firearms lawfully. Individuals who do not do so are no longer fit and proper.

A person is not considered fit and proper if:

1. They are subject to a protection order under domestic violence legislation. Protection orders have as a standard condition the 'deemed revocation' of the respondent's firearms licence. This standard condition may be discharged by a Judge on application from the respondent.
2. In the opinion of a Commissioned Officer of Police there are grounds for making such an order.
3. They have had their firearms licence revoked on the grounds they are not a fit and proper person.
4. A person who is not fit and proper is likely to have access to their firearms.
5. They fail to secure their firearms as required by the Arms Regulations 1992.
6. They demonstrate any other behavioural based problems, such as substance misuse, routine offending against the law (including the Arms Act), violence, attempted suicide and mental ill health such that it might cause concern.

Firearms licenses, endorsements and dealers licenses may be revoked where a person is considered no longer fit and proper to use or possess firearms, or as dealer they fail to exercise due control over their business.

Where Police have revoked a firearms licence they may, when the person has demonstrated themselves fit and proper reinstate the licence. A revoked firearms licence may be reinstated on appeal to the Courts.

OPERATIONAL IMPLICATIONS

The New Zealand legislative framework establishes as offences the unlawful use or possession of firearms. These are included in both arms control legislation and the criminal code.

Offences that involve the misuse of firearms, including possession for other than lawful, proper or sufficient purpose tend to be well understood. Offences involving the simple possession and transfer of firearms, in the absence of any other substantive offending require further explanation.

While they continue to hold a licence and/or endorsement a person is lawfully able to possess the categories of firearms that the licence and/or endorsement apply to[8]. It is only when they do not hold a licence and/or endorsement that a person may commit the offence of unlawful possession.

Another co-op ad with New Zealand Mountain Safety

This applies irrespective that the person may or may not have taken possession of pistols, MSSAs or restricted weapons other than with a permit to procure. The onus for ensuring that a person holds a permit to procure rests with the person supplying the pistol, MSSA or restricted weapon. The person taking possession of the pistol, MSSA or restricted weapon may be party to the offence (by aiding or procuring the breach of the Arms Act) of supplying a pistol, MSSA or restricted weapon to a person who does not hold a permit to procure, albeit that it is themselves.

If a person makes or assembles for themselves a pistol, MSSA or restricted weapon they do not commit the offences of unlawful possession or supplying a pistol, MSSA or restricted weapon to a person who does not hold a permit to procure - so long as they hold a firearms licence bearing the requisite endorsement. A wise person in these circumstances will have advised their Arms Officer that they are making or assembling the pistol, MSSA or restricted weapon, ensuring that the firearm is recorded against their licence and/or endorsement.

It is when they come to supplying the pistol, MSSA or restricted weapon to another that the person making or assembling the pistol, MSSA or restricted weapon must ensure that the person they are supplying it to holds a permit to procure.

THE DEVELOPMENT OF LEGISLATION AND POLICY - A CONSULTATIVE APPROACH

In setting the principles of modern policing in 1829 Peel stated that 'the extent to which the cooperation of the public can be secured diminishes proportionally the necessity of the use of physical force and compulsion for achieving police objectives'. One mechanism to gain public cooperation is to include them fully in the law and policy making process.

The outcome of legislation developed in a consultative process is better law and enhanced public acceptance, and ultimately compliance with that law.

In the same way it is important to include interested parties in the development of policy. The New Zealand Mountain Safety Council, as an independent organisation very focussed on safety is central to this consultative process. The Mountain Safety Council branch network of instructors is pivotal to explaining law and policy to the wider firearm using public.

It is also important to acknowledge that firearm users tend to be the good people in the community. This is especially so in rural and small town communities. They will be the same people who support Neighbourhood Support, Victim Support, youth education and other policing initiatives. They will also be the people police officers rely on for support and back up!

The development of policy in terms of arms control is based on (to quote Chief Justice, Dame Sian Elias when she opened the 2005 Criminology Conference) "solid research, not pious hopes"[9].`

DIFFERENT STATES, DIFFERENT NEEDS

Arms control internationally is agreed by instruments such as, for example the UN Programme of Action to Prevent, Combat and Eradicate the Illicit Trade in Small Arms and Light Weapons (SALW) in All Its Aspects (referred to in what follows as the 'POA').

An arms control regime is likely to be more effective if it takes into account the differing histories, cultures, environments and patterns of firearms possession and use that are apparent in different States. A 'one size fits all' approach is likely to be less effective than approaches that address these differences. The POA commits States to take steps that bear in mind the 'different situations, capacities and priorities of States and regions' (POA, II (1)).

Given this, States are justified in putting energy into developing strategies that they consider are more likely to be effective, given their own particular circumstances.

Target shooter with HK SL8

CONCLUSION

This paper has provided an overview of the New Zealand arms control, sharing with others the strengths of that regime. Arms control in New Zealand has been placed within an international context and the reason for the New Zealand view explained.

The New Zealand arms control regime can be more fully understood by referring to the following key documents:

- The Arms Act 1983
- The Arms (Restricted Weapons and Specially Dangerous Airguns) Order 1984
- The Arms Regulations 1992
- The Arms Code (Firearms Safety Manual Issued By the New Zealand Police)
- The Arms Manual 2002
- The Vetting Guide
- The Vetting Master Guide

Endnotes

1. This report was prepared by Inspector Joe Green, Manager: Licensing and Vetting of the New Zealand Police. Joe has a B.A. (Hons) and Dip. Bus. Stud. He has been a Police officer since 1983, working at all ranks in both administrative and operational roles to his current rank of Inspector. Since October 1998 he has managed the Licensing and Vetting Service Centre. This Service Centre is responsible, among other things for the national coordination of firearms control. He has advised a Parliamentary Select Committee on one Arms Amendment Bill, has developed policy which is within the Arms Manual 2002, is advising on the Arms Amendment Bill #3, has been advisor to UN delegations, and to the Australian Government in the 2007 review of its national firearms management system. He is the Police representative to the New Zealand Mountain Safety Council (NZMSC) and from 1999-2007 was the Deputy Chair of NZMSC. NZMSC is the civilian organisation responsible for the nation wide training of all firearms licence applicants. In practice this means that Joe has been associated with the design, administration and enforcement of firearms control systems on a full time basis for nine years. This is backed by operational policing experience.

2. New Zealand has a very low crime rate with firearms, being approximately 1.3% of all violent crime, a very low accidental injury and death rate, and a reducing suicide rate with firearms as the choice of method (for example, in the 15-24 age group for males, suicide by firearm decreased from 6.9 deaths per 100 000 in 1977 to 2.9 per 100 000 in 1996). The culture of firearm use in New Zealand is such that Police do not routinely carry firearms.

3. In his paper Global Deaths from Firearms (2003: page 2) David Kopel comments on statements that take on a truth of their own as 'factoids' that 'gain strength through repetition, often without any (or very slim) empirical basis'. Such factoids are apparent in both national and international discourse on arms control.

4. The cause to possess pistols and restricted weapons is determined by statute. The applicant must be a target pistol shooter (member of a club recognised by the Commissioner of Police), or a bona fide collector, or a person to whom the pistol or restricted weapon has special significance as an heirloom or memento, or the Director or Curator of a museum, or an approved employee or member of a bona fide theatre, film or television company or society. For MSSAs the applicant must satisfy Police they have reason to possess the MSSA. Most common reasons include pest destruction, competitive service rifle shooting and film production.

5. Acting on the 'direction of the Commissioner (of Police)' is an aspect of New Zealand legislation that makes it important to include Police policy, collated in the Police (Arms) Manual, as part of the overall arms control regime. In this sense New Zealand legislation is less prescriptive than some other legislative frameworks. Being less prescriptive should not be interpreted as being less restrictive.

6. The primary purpose of the permit to procure process is to ensure that the pistol, MSSA or restricted weapon is supplied only to a fit and proper person.

7. New Zealand does not have a universal registration regime. In 1983 a radical and substantial decision was made to move from a registration regime that focussed on the firearm to a comprehensive licensing regime that focussed on ensuring, as far as possible, that only fit and proper people had access to firearms. This change was made on the basis that the registration system suffered from inaccuracy, had indications of low compliance, did not assist crime prevention and detection, was of high cost with the money of maintaining such a system better spent on other essential police duties (Judge Thorp; 1997, pages 13-16 Review of Firearms Control in New Zealand). A licensing system with more intensive vetting was considered to provide effective arms control. This view has not changed and is supported by more recent international experience. Despite recommending a universal registration regime in his 1997 Review of Firearms Control in New Zealand Judge Thorp noted that in order to be effective a threshold of 90% compliance was necessary. Judge Thorp (page 178) concluded that 'at this time there is insufficient evidence to conclude that the assistance which registration would provide to crime prevention and detection would in itself support the costs involved in establishing it'. The observation of the

outcome of legislative changes in other common law jurisdictions has not encouraged New Zealand to change the 1983 decision.

8. This is a natural corollary of a system based on licensing people as 'fit and proper' to possess firearms, and certain categories of firearms (rather than a system based on a registration regime). That pistols, MSSAs or restricted weapons are, or are not recorded on Police systems has no bearing on whether or not they are lawfully, or unlawfully possessed.

9. Despite the complexity of firearm control ('requiring social and economic rather than technical solutions' (United Kingdom Home Office (2006: 1) some advocates, including operational police staff are attracted to and promote a range of mechanisms that include the universal registration of firearms, the banning of possession of certain categories of firearms, the deactivation of firearms, buybacks and the increase in penalties for the illegal possession and use of firearms. A research based approach suggests these approaches to arms control to be less than effective.

SWEDEN

A SUMMARY OF THE POSITIVE CONSEQUENCES, FOLLOWING A TRADITIONAL, PRIVATE HUNT

Christer Holmgren with translation by Carin Höglund

In the Nordic countries, and especially Sweden, Norway and Finland, hunting is a centuries old tradition that is still, contrary to other parts of Europe, deeply-rooted in large parts of the population. Historically, the reason is quite simple. The dense forestation, sparsely populated areas and harsh climate made agrarian success somewhat uncertain and an insufficient resource to support the population.

The combination of small scale farming, hunting, fishing, and trapping is still today a viable way to make a living in Sweden. While these traditions are less common today, they are simply two or three generation removed from the present urban dwellers.

Comparatively speaking in relation to its total population of nine million people, Sweden has many hunters and shooters. There are approximately 300,000 registered hunters, who purchase national hunting licences each year. A national hunting licence is required for every hunter whether or not the hunt takes place on their own land or as a guest on someone else's land. There are approximately 640,000 registered firearms owners in Sweden who own approximately 1.8 million firearms for hunting or match shooting. Despite the relatively easy availability of firearms for hunting and match shooting, they are rarely used in crime. On the contrary, crime rates are lower in areas with a large proportion of hunters.

From the left: Michael Larsson, Stefan Alesved and Anders Brolund, Sweden. They are the Swedish National Team, which won the Gold medal in the 60 Prone, in Granada, Spain in 2007.

The majority of Swedish hunters belong to the middle class and have average incomes. This is not due to the fact that hunting is an inexpensive activity in Sweden, but to the fact that the right to hunt and the right to take game is tied to the ownership of land. Furthermore, the landowner also owns the right to grant temporary or longer term authorization for another person to hunt on his piece of land or to lease it out. In principle, there is no minimum size that the land must be to be hunted. Five hectares (12 acres) are actually enough to hunting. For Moose, the hunting however is limited to a fixed number of days when you can shoot a full grown animal if the opportunity presents itself. Moose and red deer are in principle the only species where the government can regulate or limit the number of game taken down by the land owner or the lessee.

In practice, it is difficult to carry on a meaningful hunt in a small area. In parts of Sweden where hunting areas have been broken into small areas over the years, usually a voluntary hunting cooperative is created grouping parcels of land and forest together to create a game preservation district or a club or a society that allow the members to hunt over a larger territory.

A large proportion of the Swedish hunters lease their hunting right from private landowners, forestry companies or governmental institutions. The leased area, which is culled at the hunter's discretion when it comes to game preservation, with the exception of moose and red deer, varies from some ten hectares to several thousand depending upon the part of Sweden. In the North, where moose hunting is predominant, and where other species are rather scarce or non-existent, a normal hunting territory is around 3-5000 hectares for every 10-15 hunters. The lease costs are usually fairly reasonable, approximately 5-15 SEK (Swedish krona) per hectare. If the land belongs to a forestry company, local hunting teams often go on short term hunts, where in addition to a small yearly fee, they pay an additional fee for each animal brought down. The quota of game, normally moose, is regulated by the forestry company which applies for a yearly quota for its entire land area. The forestry company can determine where the hunts should take place and how many moose will be hunted in a particular area to meet the animal management requirements to promote the maximum growth of timber. In the South, where the hunt is mostly for roe deer, fallow deer, boar, and small game, the lease costs are higher per hectare. The rate is determined by the density of game, and the competition

Swedish Moose

between the hunters to find accessible hunting grounds. This is especially accentuated in densely populated areas, and most of all around the bigger cities. The lease cost can vary from 100-350 SEK per hectare, depending on game density and the areas closeness to urban areas. In Mid-Sweden or southern Sweden, 500-1000 hectares is considered to be a fairly large hunting area.

While Swedish hunters may seek animal trophies, the hunt in Sweden is still to a large extent focused on traditional life-supporting hunts, where the taking of meat for personal consumption has a high value. Up north, especially in the 1980s, when the Swedish moose population was at its highest level ever and 150-170,000 moose were brought down every year, the hunt could generate enough meat for each hunter that it would more than cover all of the costs for the hunt. Additionally since the hunting costs, particularly in the South, are expensive and the recoup of expenses through the taking of meat in unlikely, there is an emotional component to hunting which has the greatest value.

While the traditional hunt, with hunting on your own or leased grounds together with friends and associates in a bigger or smaller hunting team still dominates, commercial hunts have become more and more common in Sweden. In the North, the opportunity to hunt brown bear attracts great many sportsmen. The interest is not just from Swedish hunters, but also from our neighbouring nations. Bear is still an exotic game in Sweden and the sale of just a few days of bear hunting to a group of visiting hunters can easily finance a large part of the costs of leasing the land for your moose hunt.

There is an increased interest in hunting by urban dwellers who wish to go on short-term hunts. The explosive increase in the boar population requires greater numbers of hunters. While the regulations are stringent, it is important that hunters help manage the game. Many people, however, are not interested in the demands and commitment of being a hunter.

Road Sign

So what does hunting mean from a socio-economic perspective? In Sweden, it is common to determine the outcome of hunting based on kilograms of meat gathered as a measure of value. It is not an insignificant amount we are talking about. A study completed a few years ago, showed that annually approximately 17,000,000 kg of meat were culled at a value of close to one billion SEK. Added to this value is the recreational value, which is often said to be twice the value of the meat, where the hunting costs are considered to be included.

The question is how to look at the meat resources, from a socio-economic perspective. In practice, the meat from game mainly benefits hunters. The consumption of game decreases the number of employees that would be needed to generate by the same amount of meat from livestock for consumption. In practice, the value of game consumed by hunters is thus can be seen as a refund of costs, decreasing the hunters' expenses. The value of the work they voluntarily put in to preserve the wild game within the nation is enormous and difficult to calculate.

Sharing nature with wild animals always effects society in some way. The costs are enormous: the direct and indirect damage to growing forests, agricultural crops as well as the material damage and injuries to human beings as a result from collisions between game and vehicles. Some costs can be calculated and others only estimated such as the damage on growing forests. But undoubtedly, we are talking about several million SEK every year, despite the reduction of game through hunting.

Another issue is what additional costs for society if all private hunting was banned and game populations would be by necessity managed by government employees. The data mentioned earlier shows that there are 300,000 Swedish hunting licencees who each on average devote 26 days per year to hunting. This is the equivalent of 35,000 full time employees who would be required to bring down the same amount of game. In addition to this, hunters also help track the injured game from the approximately 35,000 collisions between game and vehicles every year in Sweden. A rough estimate suggests that it would require 50-100 full time employees every year, if all the animals could be tracked in four hours.

This number of full time employees is equivalent to the staff of a very large multinational corporation where just the salaries, including all social fees, easily cost 12-15 billion SEK per year. The additional costs of the administration, vehicles, fuel, and other equipment such as firearms and ammunition could of course be estimated but these costs are left to the imagination of the reader. If the government hunters needed to drive just 50 km per day, in connection to the pursuit of game, the fuel cost alone would reach 450 million SEK per year. A more realistic figure for the travel expenses including the depreciation of the vehicle, service, and insurance would be almost triple, or around 1.2 to 1.3 billion SEK per year. This is more than the value of the meat the hunt, approximated at one billion SEK, generated in Sweden on a yearly basis.

The socio-economical value of hunting in Sweden can be analyzed from two perspectives. The first is to assess the number of employees and the tax income received from hunters which amounts to billions of SEK through the payment for hunting ground leases, purchase of equipment, trips and transportation for the domestic hunts. The other and by far the more important aspect of the socio-economical benefit of traditional hunting in Sweden, is that society is not charged for the enormous costs that would occur if the domestic game was to be managed and taxed by central government authorities and run by salary-paid workers.

It may not be apparent to some but Swedish hunters perform an extremely valuable task for society in managing wildlife. The demands on responsible hunters are enormous when it comes to the care, protection and preservation of game and the necessity to decrease the ability of wild game to damage forests, fields and property. Hunters take this obligation seriously. Hunters should be respected, applauded and thanked for the service that they supply to society.

LEAD POLLUTION

The spread of metallic lead through Swedish hunting and civilian match shooting has been a matter of discussion and intense debates recently. This image below shows that the actual accumulation of lead from ammunition is totally negligible in comparison to atmospheric fallout from bio-absorbable lead, and the natural occurrence of lead in the upper layer of moraine.

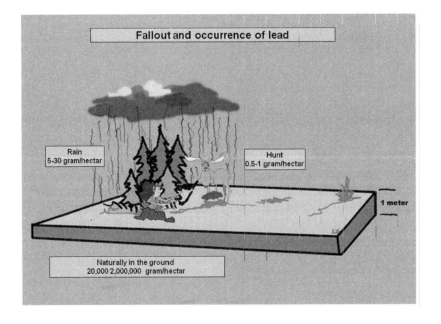

UNITED STATES

CURRENT STATUS OF HUNTING, SPORT SHOOTING AND GUN OWNERSHIP IN THE UNITED STATES

Alan Gottlieb and Dave Workman

The United States is unique to the nations of the world in that its constitution contains not only a Bill of Rights, but it lists the Right to Keep and Bear Arms second only to the rights of Free Speech, Press and Religion. It is this constitutional provision that has enabled American citizens to own firearms for a variety of purposes, including hunting, competitive and recreational shooting, gun collecting and personal protection.

American Constitutional scholars insist that the Constitution does not "grant" any rights, but merely affirms that these rights, and others, pre-existed as fundamental human rights.

Millions of American citizens own firearms solely for the purpose of self-defense, and there is research data available that suggests these armed citizens annually thwart or intervene to stop violent crimes more than 1 million times each year.

Yet there is also evidence that many of these citizens, in an effort to maintain proficiency, frequently become more active shooters, participating in various casual competitions, local club shoots and other activities.

Americans continue to be possibly the most active hunters and shooters of any western country, and millions of citizens participate in non-hunting shooting sports, including trap and skeet, Sporting Clays (a shotgun shooting activity that simulates hunting with a shotgun); rifle, shotgun and pistol competitions held on local, regional and national levels; so-called "Action Pistol" competitions that require not just concentration, but also some physical agility and speed, and the increasingly popular sport of "Cowboy Action Shooting," which has its roots in the Action Pistol competitions but adds the color of contestants dressing up in costumes one normally associates with western cinema.

There are specific types of shooting activities that are competitive in nature, not the least of which are the muzzle loader competitions, traditionally called "Rendezvous" in a remembrance of the annual gatherings of fur trappers and traders in the early 1800s in what is now the western United States, but was then an untamed and uncivilized wilderness.

These competitions are rooted deeply in the American tradition. Historically, dating back to the colonial period prior to the founding of the United States as a nation, residents of the various settlements

gathered on occasion to demonstrate their shooting prowess with commonly-owned arms of the day, flintlock rifles and pistols. At that time, skill with a rifle was not simply something to be admired, but also necessary for one's survival, as hunting was a matter of subsistence and survival, especially on the American frontier, and the American hunter had but a single shot with which to either hit his mark or go hungry.

Today, of course, tradition continues to bring millions of American citizens to shooting ranges and hunting camps, gun shows – where participants will buy and sell firearms and accessories, discuss firearm maintenance, safety and repair, hold classes on firearm safety for the general public, and frequently discuss firearms politics as they relate to both national and even international current events – and other public forums where shooting and gun ownership may be involved.

Of course, all of this shooting activity reinforces the international image of Americans as being steeped in a so-called "gun culture," and in many ways – all of them positive – that is certainly the case. However, one should not confuse the images seen on television and theater screens with American firearms owners.

By some estimates that are considered to be reasonably accurate, there are between 80 and 90 million gun owners in the United States, and they own upwards of 230 million firearms of all types and descriptions. While some of those firearms are held in collections simply for their historical or artistic value, the majority of firearms owned in the United States today are what Americans casually refer to as "working guns." That is, these are guns that are used at gun ranges, for hunting, casual shooting, competition and personal protection.

Just a look at membership in various firearms organizations paints a stunning portrait. The National Rifle Association (www.nra.org) has some 4 million members, while the Citizens Committee for the Right to Keep and Bear Arms (www.ccrkba.org) boasts some 600,000 members and supporters, the Second Amendment Foundation (www.saf.org) reports approximately 650,000 members, and smaller organizations including Gun Owners of America also have a few hundred thousand members.

Add to that the hundreds of thousands of sportsmen who belong to various hunting and wildlife conservation organizations, local gun clubs and state-level firearms politics organizations, and one really only touches the surface of the American firearms community.

American firearms owners come from all walks of life, racial and ethnic groups, political and social groups, and they represent virtually all professions from scientists and doctors, to attorneys, police and military, businessmen and women, politicians, farmers, construction workers, pilots, engineers, actors and performers, educators and students. There is no single stereotype that fits what one might call the "typical American gun owner."

According to data compiled by the National Shooting Sports Foundation (www.nssf.org) – an American firearms trade organization based in the state of Connecticut – hunters and recreational shooters in the United States spend an estimated $24.7 billion annually on firearms, ammunition and related equipment including clothing, optics, reloading supplies and equipment for manufacturing their own ammunition, and other accessories.

Early in the 20th Century, the United States Congress passed a law that placed a 10 percent federal excise tax on handguns andan 11 percent excise tax on rifles and shotguns, and ammunition, the revenues from which are annually distributed to natural resources agencies in each of the states for the purpose of preserving and enhancing wildlife populations and habitat, and teaching firearm and hunting safety to millions of young Americans. More than $163 million is annually apportioned to the state wildlife agencies, and since the law was passed in 1937, more than $4 billion has been raised by this program.

In 2006, the most recent year for which data is available, more than 31.7 million American citizens participated in at least one shooting-related sport, according to the NSSF, which used data from the 2006 American Sports Data, Superstudy of Sports Participation.

The federal Bureau of Alcohol, Tobacco, Firearms and Explosives currently estimates that one out of every two homes in the United States contains at least one firearm.

Of particular interest to economists and employment specialists, data suggests that the hunting and shooting-related industries employ more people in America than are employed at all of the stores operated by Sears, one of the largest retail chains in the country.

HUNTING PARTICIPATION

The hunting tradition runs deep in the United States, with two or three generations of families often participating in hunting together as an annual rite. However, over the past 30 years, participation has shown a gradual decline.

In 1975, for example, figures from the U.S. Fish & Wildlife Service, a branch of the federal Department of Interior that manages the nation's wildlife refuge system and monitors migratory bird populations among its duties, there were 16,597,807 licensed hunters. They purchased an impressive 24,618,619 hunting licenses, game tags, permits and migratory waterfowl stamps.

It is not unusual in the United States that hunters will travel from one state to another in pursuit of game, both for the meat and for trophies. They must purchase separate state hunting licenses and game harvest permits or tags on these trips.

By the year 2000, however, the number of hunters had declined to 15,044,324 according to Fish & Wildlife Service figures, but that smaller number of hunters purchased 29,977,392 licenses, game tags, permits and stamps, so it appears that while participation in hunting had declined, those who participated did so more actively.

Duck hunter and companion

By 2006, the number of hunters in the United States had declined farther, to an estimated 12.5 million who were age 16 or older, according to the most recent hunting survey by the Fish & Wildlife Service. However, data compiled by the Service from the states indicated that 14,575,484 hunters purchased 32,620,175 hunting licenses, game tags, permits and stamps, and they spent an estimated $22.9 billion on their activities. Of that number, an estimate 10.7 million hunters pursued big game alone.

Thirty-five percent of the big game hunters pursued their quarry on public land, and in that arena, the United States excels. There are hundreds of millions of acres of public land in the United States,

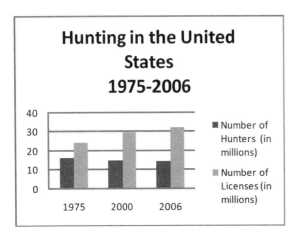

much of it in national forests, national wildlife refuges and national recreation areas. Other public lands open to hunting are owned or managed by the Bureau of Land Management and other federal and state agencies.

Statistically, hunting in the United States is dominated by men, with 11.4 million male hunters reported in 2006, as opposed to 1.2 million women who hunted. The largest single age group participating was in the 35-to-44 year range, with 3.1 million. The next largest group is in the 45-to-54 year age range, with 2.9 million.

Recruitment does not appear to be keeping up with the aging population of hunters. In 2006, the Fish & Wildlife Service reported only 500,000 hunters ages 16 and 17, and 1 million in the 18-to-24 year age range. That number is surpassed by hunters in the 55-to-64 year group, whose numbers totaled 1.9 million in 2006.

The number of licensed hunters has declined, but according to the National Shooting Sports Foundation, more than 19 million Americans annually participate in some kind of target shooting activity. Naturally, there will be some cross-over between the hunter and target shooter numbers, as serious hunters quite often will be found at gun ranges shooting targets and perhaps even participating in some type of competition.

RECRUITMENT AND RETENTION

Serious efforts are underway with a number of organizations providing programs to both recruit and retain shooters and hunters. The National Rifle Association of America – known perhaps best internationally for its political activities in defense of firearm owners' rights – has long been known within the United States as "the Red Cross of firearms safety."

The NRA maintains an active cadre of tens of thousands of certified volunteer firearms safety instructors who are trained to teach gun safety and marksmanship courses across the United States. They have trained millions of Americans in all age groups in the safe and proper use of rifles, shotguns and handguns, and many of those citizens have become active in target and recreational shooting activities at local shooting ranges.

It was under the NRA's leadership that the hunter education program was originated in the state of New York in 1949, and in the 59 years since that program first began teaching firearm safety to new hunters, state wildlife resource agencies have assumed responsibility for the program and have trained millions of American youth in the safe handling of firearms.

This program has grown to require the creation of the International Hunter Education Association, which now promotes hunter safety programs on an international scale.

Other organizations have developed over the years, including Youth Shooting Sports Alliance (www.youthshootingsa.com), whose mission is to "provide leadership in the development and promotion of family-friendly shooting range facilities to encourage continued participation in the shooting sports."

In 2007, YSSA conducted a needs assessment designed to identify areas in which the program could grow if facilities and equipment were available. In early 2008, YSSA began conducting a series of community forums designed to improve shooting opportunities. These Shooter Retention Forums were day-long events in various communities that identified various opportunities and explained the importance of good relations between shooting ranges and the communities they serve to develop a positive image and atmosphere for families.

The National Shooting Sports Foundation has developed a program called "First Shots," aimed at

Youth Shooting Sport Association

recruiting new shooters who will join mentors to fire their first shots, which hopefully will bring them into the sport. In 2008, nearly 100 shooting ranges across the United States are scheduled to host First Shots events, where participants will have the opportunity to try their hand at shooting rifles, shotguns and handguns. Some 20 different companies and organizations support this effort, which is seen as augmenting similar programs conducted by the NRA and its local affiliate shooting organizations in the 50 states.

There is a website devoted to this program: www.firstshots.org.

Another effort aimed at preserving and enhancing shooting sports is conducted by the U.S. Sportsman's Alliance under the auspices of the Outdoor Business Council. Participants include leaders in the shooting and firearms industry, and their mission is to work toward preserving and expanding hunting and shooting opportunities, and assist wildlife management programs. This group is chaired by Tommy Millner, president and CEO of the Remington Firearms company. Information is available at: www.ussportsmen.org.

SAFETY BENEFITS, SUCCESS STORIES

While international news coverage of firearms events in the United States tends to focus on either court cases such as the one challenging a handgun ban in the nation's capitol as an infringement on the Second Amendment of the U.S. Constitution's Bill of Rights, or on tragedies such as the mass shooting in April 2007 at Virginia Tech, there are untold success stories in the shooting community.

According to the National Shooting Sports Foundation, (www.nssf.org) accidental firearm-related fatalities in the U.S. are at their lowest point since record-keeping began, according to an NSSF report, using data from the National Safety Council's Injury Facts Report for 2007.

Firearms accidents have declined 77 percent from 1930, the first year data was kept. In 2005, there were only 730 accidental firearm fatalities in the United States.

Thanks to the hunter education program mentioned earlier, hunting has become one of the safest recreational activities in the nation, with a decline of more than 50 percent in the number of fatal hunting accidents between 1995 and 2005. During that same period, according to the International Hunter Education Association's Hunting Incident Summary, non-fatal accidents fell by 60 percent.

The combined efforts of hunter education program instructors and National Rifle Association volunteer instructors has led to a significant decline in firearms mishaps. The accident rate with firearms is far lower than accidental deaths due to auto accidents, drownings, burns, poisonings and ingestion of food or other objects, according to the National Safety Council.

Another "success story" that is perhaps under-advertised by America's shooting industry is the creation of USA Shooting, an organization headquartered in Colorado Springs, Colorado. It is here that the United States Olympic Shooting Team trains, and the facility also holds seminars, and provides camps and facilities for local clubs.

Young shooter at 2008 Junior Olympic Championships (C) USA Shooting

It is the largest indoor shooting facility in the Western Hemisphere, according to their website: www.usashooting.com.

Constructed in 1985, the facility is used by 25 resident and day-use athletes for Olympics training. There are three separate ranges with a total of 29 firing points from 50 meters and another 73 firing points from 10 meters. In addition, outdoor ranges at the International Shooting Park include four superimposed international-style skeet and bunker trap fields, shade shelters and a clubhouse, according to USA Shooting's website.

On a local level, there are examples of recruitment activities that promote shooting and firearm safety. The National Shooting Sports Foundation's "Scholastic Clay Target Program" is one such venture, which has found considerable popularity, not to mention positive media attention, wherever it goes.

While firearms are typically prohibited on America's public school grounds, these shooting programs recruit the assistance of local gun ranges and NRA-certified firearms instructors. Participants pass a hunter education course.

In the State of Michigan, according to a report from the National Shooting Sports Foundation early in 2008, a new law allowed parents to take their children or other newcomers hunting under what is called the "apprentice hunting program." During its first year, Michigan's Department of Natural Resources reported that 14,558 apprentice hunters went afield prior to completing a hunter education course. In 2007, that number increased to 16,389 participants.

According to the National Shooting Sports Foundation, there are now 24 states that have passed laws similar to the apprentice program in Michigan, so there should be considerable expansion of the program in the years ahead.

All of this was possible under the Families Afield program that was created by NSSF in cooperation with the National Wild Turkey Federation and U.S. Sportsman's Alliance.

CONSERVATION GROUPS

American sportsmen and women are passionate about their sport and together they have annually raised tens of millions of dollars that support wildlife management and enhancement projects across the United States. Through banquets and raffles, contribution programs and other fund-raising efforts, organizations including the Rocky Mountain Elk Foundation, Mule Deer Foundation, National Wild Turkey  Federation, Ducks Unlimited, Delta Waterfowl (www.deltawaterfowl.org), Pheasants Forever/ Quail Forever (www.pheasantsforever.org), Ruffed Grouse Society (www.ruffedgrousesociety.org), Foundation for North American Wild Sheep (www.fnaws.org) and others have purchased or leased tens of millions of acres of critical wildlife habitat, from ranch lands adjacent to national forests or other public lands which provide prime habitat for big game, to prairie potholes where ducks and geese annual nest, these efforts supplement, and sometimes even surpass, projects mounted by state and federal fish and wildlife agencies.

 Members of these organizations are devoted shooters and hunters who have assumed leadership roles in their communities on issues that include shooting range protection and construction of new ranges, support for hunter education programs and mentoring projects, habitat improvement work and more.

Quite often, support for these fund raising efforts come from firearm manufacturers, who donate guns to be raffled off at fund-raising events. Additionally, other manufacturers of shooting accessories will support these programs with donations of goods, and hunting guides often contribute hunting opportunities for high bidders.

A common thread among these organizations is that they were started by hunters; people who actually participate in the specific sport they are working to preserve and enhance, along with the tradition they envision passing on to future generations.

For example, since its creation in 1973, the National Wild Turkey Federation (www.nwtf.org) has helped accelerate a program that started in the 1950s under which state and provincial wildlife agencies have transplanted roughly 200,000 wild turkeys of various species to new habits across the United States. These new bird populations have thrived, to the point that there are now more than 7 million wild turkeys in North America, from Canada to Mexico.

Ducks Unlimited (www.ducks.org) has announced an effort to raise at least $1.7 billion for wetlands habitat conservation under a program it calls "Wetlands for Tomorrow," which should provide for future waterfowl hunting opportunities for generations to come.

Pheasants Forever (www.pheasantsforever.org) chapters have completed more than 27,000 different habitat projects since the organization was founded in 1982. These projects have benefited more than 4 million acres, and the organization has acquired some 100,000 acres of habitat.

Likewise, the Mule Deer Foundation (www.muledeer.org) has endeavored to preserve and enhance critical mule deer habitat across the western United States. Founded in 1988, this 10,000-member organization has some 80 chapters nationwide and their mission is to restore lost habitat and revive the mule deer herds, which have been declining for the past several years.

And the Rocky Mountain Elk Foundation (www.rmef.org) has a long history of raising millions of dollars at regional banquets and auctions that support habitat improvement and land acquisition projects, along with elk re-introduction programs in several states. RMEF today is one of the nation's largest private conservation organizations made up of hunters. Since its creation in 1985, the RMEF has raised more than $185 million for its programs. The organization has more than 550 chapters across the United States with some 160,000 members.

SHOOTING RANGES

Public shooting ranges have been under steady threat from expanding urbanization in the United States. Lands that were once rural and remote enough to provide acreage for developed and undeveloped shooting ranges is now being converted to suburban residential development at an increasing.

While some state legislatures have passed laws that protect existing shooting ranges from closure through local political pressure, other states have not protected their gun ranges in such a way.

While outdoor shooting ranges have suffered from human encroachment, private businesses have developed over the years in the heart of metropolitan areas that cater to shooters by constructing indoor shooting ranges. Such facilities are typically limited to 25- and perhaps 50-yard shooting areas, and they may also limit the types of firearms that may be used, they do at least provide shooting opportunities to urban firearms owners without the necessity of traveling several miles to a remote area.

An added benefit of such indoor range facilities is that they typically offer educational opportunities for new gun owners. Rarely does such an indoor range not have classes that are conducted by certified instructors, and the few that do not have such on-site courses available typically can refer prospective students to instructors in their areas.

Indoor gun ranges are invariably operated in conjunction with retail firearms outlets, allowing customers to not only buy firearms, but to also shoot them. Many of these facilities offer rental guns for use on their ranges, allowing new shooters or experienced gun owners to sample new and different gun models prior to making a purchase.

The advent of such shooting ranges has given rise in the United States to a "cottage industry" that develops state-of-the-art ventilation systems, to prevent shooters from breathing air saturated with lead particles and gunpowder residue. Another "cottage industry" that has developed in conjunction with indoor shooting ranges involves the development of insulation materials and strategies to reduce the noise generated by gunshots fired indoors, so shooting does not disrupt the neighborhood in which these indoor gun ranges are established.

While such gun ranges have not become as widespread as one might imagine in a nation where private firearms ownership is so high, such facilities are appearing in more communities. Their presence can often help to remove the stigma that seems to have developed over the past 40 years toward firearms and shooting in many American cities. And, as increasing numbers of American citizens are drawn to indoor gun ranges for the first time, millions of those new shooters change their attitudes about firearms ownership, thus helping to "turn the tide" that once threatened to abolish the shooting sports in the United States.

Indoor gun ranges are operated by private businessmen who are, perhaps above all else, entrepreneurs, and they frequently create "shooting leagues" at their range facilities as a way to attract new business. Others might hold "Ladies' nights" that are geared specifically toward females to not only introduce new shooters, but provide them with a comfortable environment in which they do not feel the pressure to compete against typically more experienced male shooters. Quite often, the participants in such activities are first drawn to shooting sports by the educational opportunities offered at such ranges.

While increasing numbers of women are purchasing firearms in America today, the gun of choice is typically a handgun, purchased for personal protection. That initial purchase, however, often leads to a secondary purchase of a handgun more suitable to target shooting and competition.

A surprising number of women purchase handguns to carry while they are hiking and backpacking in America's wilderness areas, and they frequently become skilled marksmen through regular practice at indoor or outdoor shooting ranges.

These indoor gun ranges may also host seminars featuring factory representatives from various firearm manufacturers, and they will provide opportunities to sample new products and discuss different firearm models. Such events are known to attract hundreds of gun owners and prospective purchasers, and are yet one more strategy used by private businessmen to increase their retail traffic by creating new customers.

CONCLUSION

American gun owners and the industry that serves them have become a political force in the United States, as they have recognized that it is in the political arena where the future of shooting sports and hunting will be determined. While the United States may be somewhat unique to the world in terms of the number of citizens who hunt, shoot, collect and use firearms for various activities, it is not alone as a nation where citizens have grown to enjoy and appreciate their firearms traditions.

NOTES

Photos credits: page 37, *Women & Guns Magazine;* page. 39, Alex Langbell, Columbia Basin Waterfowl, (509)728-0145: page 41 provided courtesy of the Youth Shooting Sports Alliance; page 42, USA Shooting. All Logos are property of their respective owners.

Further Reading

Ayoob, Massad.. 1980. *In the Gravest Extreme.* Police Bookshelf.

Cottrol, Robert. 1994. *Gun Control and the Constitution: Sources and Explorations of the Second Amendment.* Routeledge.

Cramer, Clayton E. 2007. *Armed In America: The Remarkable Story Of How and Why Guns Became as American as Apple Pie.* Thomas Nelson.

Dizard, Jan E. 2003. *Mortal Stakes: Hunters and Hunting in Contemporary America.* University of Massachusetts Press.

Gottlieb, Alan M. and Dave Workman. 2008. *America Fights Back.* Bellevue: Merril Press.

Halbrook, Stephen P. 2008. *The Founders' Second Amendment: Origins of the Right to Keep and Bear Arms.* Ivan R. Dee.

Hardy, David T. 1986. *Origins and Developments of the Second Amendment.* Blacksmith Corporation.

Kates, Don B., Jr.. 1979. *Restricting Handguns: The Liberal Sceptics Speak Out.* North River Press.

Kleck, Gary. 1997. *Targeting Guns: Firearms and Their Control.* Aldine de Gruyter.

Kopel, David B. 1992. *The Samurai, the Mountie and the Cowboy: Should America Adopt the Gun Control of Other Democracies.* Prometheus.

Lott, John R., Jr. 2000. *More Guns Less Crime.* Chicago: University of Chicago Press.

Malcolm, Joyce Lee. 1994. *To Keep and Bear Arms: The Origins of an Anglo-American Right.* Cambridge: Harvard University Press.

Stange,, Mary Zeiss. 1997. *Woman the Hunter.* Boston: Beacon Press.

Young, David. 1995. *The Origin of the Second Amendment: A Documentary History of the Bill of Rights in Commentaries on Liberty, Free Government & an Armed Populace 1787-1792.* Golden Oak Books.

THE COLLECTING OF FIREARMS

2

AN HISTORICAL PERSPECTIVE

Stephen A. Petroni and David Penn

Over the last few centuries the collecting of firearms has moved from a narrow aesthetic appreciation of a relatively small number of 'firearms as art' to a broad interest in all types of arms in their wider social and historical context. The aim of this brief study is to analyse the development of collecting and collectors' efforts in preserving a vital element of our common heritage in the face of changing legislation in Europe.

EARLY COLLECTING

Before the 19th century, most collections of firearms tended to be unconscious agglomerations, as arms were superceded and relegated to display. Where firearms were consciously collected, they were often acquired as trophies of war, or as brand-new examples of technological wizardry with which to amaze one's friends, or as superb examples of decorative art (artists of the first rank, including Durer and Holbein, were involved in the decoration of weapons) or the gunsmith's skill.

THE 19TH AND 20TH CENTURIES

During the 19th century there burgeoned a serious antiquarian and scholarly interest in firearms. At first, this concentrated on arms of the highest quality, often magnificently embellished, and its viewpoint and terms of reference stemmed from the fine and decorative arts.

The 19th century was of course a time of intense technological innovation, beginning with the flintlock muzzle loader and ending with firearms technology and cartridge designs still in use today. This

Navy Luger 06

evolution itself began to be studied and collected, particularly as the increasing scarcity in the market and rising prices of the older 'armes de luxe' priced them beyond the means of all but the rich.

The growth of literacy and the popular study of history in the later 19th century also engendered an interest in firearms not for their aesthetic appeal but for their historical and personal associations, the sensation of 'shaking hands with history'. This was hardly surprising as gunpowder ranks along with the wheel, the printing press and the personal computer in its influence on society. Such studies view the firearm in terms of its use, rather than as a passive object, and therefore give far more attention to its ammunition and ballistics, for a firearm considered in isolation from its ammunition tells only half the story.

This has resulted in recent years both in a growth in the study and collection of ammunition, and, on occasion, the wish among collectors to fire an arm, if only once, to establish performance. As 'better' arms are studied intensively and the published literature about them grows, so their financial value tends to rise. Some collectors and students of arms therefore move, in quality terms, down market to consider cheap, commonly distributed arms, often in their manufacturing or social context (where such widely distributed arms have an impact far more significant than the rare arme de luxe), for the concepts of mass production and interchangeability of parts sprang from the arms industry. Such studies often involve the need to inspect large numbers of specimens of manufactured types to establish product evolution.

THE LAW AND THE COLLECTOR

As most European countries made serious attempts to control the ownership of firearms during the 1920s and 30s (itself in part a result of the widening of governments' active involvement in and control over their citizens' lives and activities during the First World War) the great majority considered it expedient to place outside the licensing system those firearms which by virtue of their age and obsoleteness were not likely to be used for their original prime utilitarian function and which were perceived as a minimal threat to society.

FESAC chairman Stephen Petroni and Secretary Roger Cook at the EU parliament in Strasbourg, France

At this period, most legislation introduced the concept of an 'antique' firearm but did not precisely define it. Nor did most legislation of the pre-war period specifically address the question of collecting more 'modern' arms (broadly 'breech loading' rather than 'muzzle loading' arms, although many early breech loading systems, such as the 'pin fire' were obsolete or fast becoming so by the 1920s) subject to licensing, and collectors were left to fit, as best they could, within the broad framework of national legislation.

During the 1970s several European countries attempted either to ban or severely tighten controls over the collecting of more 'modern' firearms as part of a wider tightening up of controls. These included the UK's Green Paper of 1973, the Finnish attempt to introduce a law modelled on that of

Sweden in 1974 and the (subsequently liberalised) Italian law of 18 April 1975. These measures were introduced against the background of urban terrorism and of a 1971 Council of Europe proposal to harmonise firearms controls to combat criminal violence.

THE GROWTH OF COLLECTORS' ORGANISATIONS

The national attempts at limiting collecting by and large foundered, but they did precipitate an increased banding-together of collectors and the founding of national collectors organisations (such as the Historical Breechloading Smallarms Association in the UK, where the interests of collectors of muzzle loaders were already met by the Muzzle Loaders' Association of Great Britain and the Arms and Armour Society).

These legislative initiatives also raised the issue of the National Heritage, with the collectors receiving the support of museums. Museums made clear their own inability, because of lack of resources, to act as the sole repository of a nation's heritage of arms, and supported the role of the responsible collector as an important part of the guardianship of the heritage. This position was endorsed by IAMAM (the International Association of Museums of Arms and Military History, now ICOMAM, an ICOM Committee) in their submission concerning the draft of the 1991 Directive. It should be noted that this view of the heritage is not restricted to arms, and the concept of a single national collection is growing, but with the artefacts physically located in both public and private collections. In the UK this is well developed in the fields of historic ships and aircraft.

This development of national organisations for firearms collectors has resulted in a much better understanding and acceptance of the benign role of the collector among governments and police. Since the mid-1970s, this acceptance of collectors has more frequently been reflected in legislation which takes account of their activities. Indeed Article 2 of the 1991 Directive specifically places outside its scope "…collectors and bodies concerned with the cultural and historical aspects of weapons and recognised as such by the Member States in whose territory they are establishes".

THE SUPRA-NATIONAL DIMENSION & FESAC

www.fesac.eu

Given the regional nature of much legislation within Europe, the establishment of FESAC, the Foundation for European Societies of Arms Collectors, represented a natural progression in the development of measures to protect and preserve the rich heritage of arms in Europe.

The Foundation for European Societies of Arms Collectors was founded in 1996 in order to influence firearms legislation and regulations in the European Union as well as to assist national organisations lobby their politicians and bureaucrats with the aim of drafting sensible legal and regulatory approaches to the legitimate ownership of collectible firearms.

National collector societies make up the membership of FESAC. However each country is allocated one seat and its delegate holds one vote. A conference is held annually to elect the members of the Board and to set the objectives and work plan for the next twelve months. The Chairman is elected by the country delegates. The current FESAC chairman is Stephen Petroni, who is also President of the Association of Maltese Arms Collectors and Shooters - AMACS - which gained considerable praise for its success in lobbying for and drafting the recently introduced Arms Act 2005 in Malta.

THE EU ARMS DIRECTIVE AMENDMENTS OF 2008

The Foundation submitted its proposals during the various stages of eighteen months of consultation and drafting during which it was in regular contact with Rapporteur Mrs. Gisela Kallenbach.

FESAC is particularly satisfied with the affirmation of the EU's recognition of the legitimate activities of individual collectors and officially recognised bodies that are concerned with the historical and cultural aspects of firearms' and the retention of the exempt status of these collectors and recognised bodies to the 1991 rules on the acquisition and possession of firearms by such persons.

This means that the provisions of the Directive do not apply to collectors and Member States are therefore free to legislate in favour of recognised collectors and grant them the possibility to acquire and preserve for posterity any type of firearm intended for collection and research purposes.

FESAC national club presidents at their annual meeting during 2007 in the Netherlands.

ECONOMIC IMPACT

THE INTERNATIONAL ECONOMIC IMPACT OF SHOOTING SPORTS

Mark Barnes[1]

Often lost in the debate over firearm ownership and use are the many benefits that the firearm industry provides to the international economy. Hunting and sport shooting are major recreational activities in the United States and around the world. According to the World Forum on the Future of Sport Shooting Activities (WFSA), there were an estimated 70 million hunters and sport shooters in the world in 1998. Most of these (67%) were in the United States and the European Union.[2] As a result of the worldwide participation, the shooting sports industry has a global economic impact through the manufacture of firearms, the international trade of firearms, and the retail sales in the industry. Certainly one must concede the significant economic benefits the industry. These economic benefits can be divided into three major categories: job creation, product revenue and international sport tourism. Each of these benefits will be examined in detail in this article.

The shooting sports industry is a significant producer of jobs internationally. In 2006, the firearms industry accounted for approximately 593,000 jobs in the United States alone.[3] According the National Shooting Sports Foundation (NSSF), there are more than 1,100 manufacturers, 100 distributors and 14,000 retailers that rely on the hunting and shooting sports industry in the United States.[4] For some perspective on these employment totals, the hunting and shooting related industries in the United States employ more people than Chrysler, Phillip Morris, United Parcel Service and Ford combined.[5] Internationally the shooting sports industry is also a major employer. For example, in the United Kingdom, there are about 70,000 jobs from the industry.[6] In the US and the European Union in 2000, there were about 1600 private companies producing firearms, 95% of which employ less than 50 employees. The major other countries in the world that employ people in the production of firearms are Brazil, China, Canada, Japan and the countries of the former USSR.[7] This shows that the industry is not just made up of large corporate gun manufacturers, but shooting sports also supports small business around the world. In the western world, the shooting sports industry accounts for an estimated 1.2 million jobs.[8]

The jobs in the industry are not limited to the manufacture and sale of firearms. Every time a hunter takes a trip into the field, there are a variety of businesses that benefit from his trip. He will need lodging if the trip spans a few days, as well as food and other supplies. Some hunters employ guides to accompany them on the trip, and novices to the shooting sports may hire instructors. Some corporations organize hunting and target shooting trips for their employees. Many businesses benefit from the travel sometimes involved in the shooting sports industry. There are an innumerable amount of jobs that are supported by the shooting sports industry outside of the manufacture of firearms.

The shooting sports industry is also responsible for generating considerable amounts of revenue from the retail sales of firearms. In the United States alone in 2006, the industry generated over twenty-four billion dollars in revenue from hunting related activities. These activities include transportation, lodging and purchases of ammunition and new firearms. According to the WFSA, the total for all shooting sports activities is about 30.9 billion dollars in the United States for 2006. Each participant in the shooting sports industry in the US spent an average of 824 dollars in 2006. In the European Union participants in the industry spent 16.4 billion dollars, which is about 1800 US dollars per participant. The total known expenditures for the industry worldwide are 55.4 billion dollars. This figure is much lower than the actual value because it can be hard to collect such data outside of the Unites States and the European Union.

The retail sales of firearms also have a large impact on the international economy through importing and exporting. The United States and the European Union are by far the largest exporters of non-military firearms. The United States in 2006 exported over 381,000 small arms, which was increase from the 260,000 small arms exported from the US in 2000.[9] In 2000, the EU exported over 839,163 units of sport shooting firearms. In that year, the other major exporters were Brazil, China, Russia, Canada, and Japan.[10] Of the firearms that are produced outside of the United States and the European Union, about 72% have a destination of the United States and the European Union, making them the largest market for such firearms.[11]

The manufacture and sales of sporting firearms have other ancillary benefits. For example, in the United States there are several taxes that are placed on the industry. The excise tax placed on manufacturers for handguns, long guns and ammunition generated over 224 million dollars in revenue in the United States. These revenues were then placed in the Pittman-Robinson Wildlife Fund, which is distributed to the states for conservation and education purposes. Conservation of the world's natural wildlife resources is not just vital to hunters, but it also benefits everyone else.

Hunters and sport shooters travel internationally for their sport. Their international tourism supports many businesses world wide. In the United States, for example, the economic impact of this kind of tourism is felt the strongest in small towns, which rely on the increase of consumer traffic that comes with hunting seasons. For some of these small towns, their economic viability depends upon sport shooters.[12] According to Fortune magazine, "The dollars spent by hunters pack special oomph, because they hit small towns far off the interstate. There, merchants look to hunting season the way Macy's looks to Christmas: it can make or break the year."[13]

The international economic impact of hunting and sport shooting is clear. For the major markets in the US and the European Union for sport shooting and hunting, the manufacture, sale, import and export of shooting sports firearms and the tourism associated with these sports has a significant economic impact. These activities have a multiplier effect that creates an even larger impact on the international economy. The jobs created in the industry provide the livelihoods to millions of people around the world, and everyone, even those not involved in the industry of sport shooting enjoy the benefits of the conservation funds generated by taxation. Often hidden in the controversy surrounding the international market for firearms are all of these economic benefits, but despite the fact that they are not well known, these economic impacts still have a major impact on the international community.

Endnotes

1. Counsel to the Firearms Importers Roundtable Trade Group (FAIR), a U.S. industry trade group.

2. WFSA, "Hunters and Sportshooters in the World," p.2

3. Association of Fish and Wildlife Agency, "Hunting in America: An Economic Powerhouse," 2007, p. 5

4. "Market Size and Economic Impact of the Sporting Firearms and Ammunition Industry in America," SAAMI, <http://www.saami.org/docs/222.pdf>. p. 2

5. Association of Fish and Wildlife Agency, "Hunting in America: An Economic Powerhouse," 2007, p. 5

 "Market Size and Economic Impact of the Sporting Firearms and Ammunition Industry in America," SAAMI, <http://www.saami.org/docs/222.pdf>. p.4

6. PACEC, "Shooting Sports: Findings of an Economic and Environmental Survey," p. 8, www.base.org/uk/media/pacec.glossyll.pdf

7. WFSA, "Hunters and Sportshooters in the World," p. 4

8. WFSA, "Hunters and Sportshooters in the World," p. 8

9. NSSF, "Industry Intelligence Reports," 2007 Edition, p.11

10. WFSA, "Hunters and Sportshooters in the World," p. 4

11. WFSA, "Hunters and Sportshooters in the World," p. 2

12. Market Size and Economic Impact of the Sporting Firearms and Ammunition Industry in America," SAAMI, <http://www.saami.org/docs/222.pdf>. p. 2

13. Market Size and Economic Impact of the Sporting Firearms and Ammunition Industry in America," SAAMI, <http://www.saami.org/docs/222.pdf>. p. 2

HISTOGRAPHY

GUN CONTROL IN ENGLAND:
THE TARNISHED GOLD STANDARD

Joyce Lee Malcolm

Upon the passage of The Firearms Act (No. 2) in 1997, British Deputy Home Secretary Alun Michael boasted: "Britain now has some of the toughest gun laws in the world." The Act was second handgun control measure passed that year, imposed a near-complete ban on private ownership of handguns, capping nearly eighty years of increasing firearms restrictions. Driven by an intense public campaign in the wake of the shooting of schoolchildren in Dunblane, Scotland, Parliament had been so zealous to outlaw all privately-owned handguns that it rejected proposals to exempt Britain's Olympic target-shooting team and handicapped target-shooters from the ban. While the government might concede that "changes to statutory law" could not "prevent criminals from gaining access to guns," the government insisted such legislation would make it more difficult for potential offenders to get guns and would "shift the balance substantially in the interest of public safety." Britain now had what was touted as "the gold standard" of gun control.

I. RISING VIOLENT CRIME

The result of the ban has been costly. Thousands of weapons were confiscated at great financial cost to the public. Hundreds of thousands of police hours were devoted to the task. But in the six years since the 1997 handgun ban, crimes with the very weapons banned have more than doubled, and firearm crime has increased markedly. In 2002, for the fourth consecutive year, gun crime in England and Wales rose—by 35 percent for all firearms, and by a whopping 46 percent for the banned handguns. Nearly 10,000 firearms offences were committed. The shootings in a single week in the fall of 2003—of a Liverpool football player and two other men in a bar, of three men in a drive-by attack in Reading, of a 32-year-old builder leaving a health club in Hertfordshire, of a 64-year-old woman trying to protect her daughter during a Nottinghamshire burglary—provoked Oliver Letwin, shadow home secretary, to remark: "One might have thought that this was Baghdad. In fact it's Blair's Britain."

At the annual conference in May, British police chiefs were warned that gun crime in the UK was growing "like a cancer." They already knew. For the first time in their history some police units are now routinely armed. American policemen have been hired to advise the British police. Clearly since the ban criminals have not found it difficult to get guns and the balance has not shifted in the interest of public safety.

Armed crime is only one part of an increasingly lawless English environment. According to Scotland Yard, in the four years from 1991 to 1995 crimes against the person in England's inner cities increased by 91 percent. In the four years from 1997 to 2001 the rate of violent crime more than doubled. The UK murder rate for 2002 was the highest for a century.

The startling crime rate increases are not the result of a low starting point. British crime rates are high compared to those of other developed nations. A recent study of all the countries of western Europe has found that in 2001 Britain had the worst record for killings, violence and burglary, and its citizens had one of the highest risks in the industrialized world of becoming victims of crime. Offences of violence in the UK were three times the level of the next worst country in western Europe, burglaries at nearly twice the next-worst level. The results are in line with the findings of a United Nations study of eighteen industrialized countries, including the United States, published in July 2002. The UN study found England and Wales at the top of the Western world's crime league, with the worst record for "very serious" offences and nearly 55 crimes per 100 people. The government insists things are improving but, as Letwin pointed out, "One thing which no amount of statistical manipulation can disguise is that violent crime has doubled in the last six years and continues to rise alarmingly."

The comparison with the United States is especially interesting because people who support gun restrictions are fond of contrasting England's strict gun laws and low rate of violent crime with America's, where there are an estimated 200 million private firearms and where 37 states now have shall issue laws that allow law-abiding residents to carry a concealed weapon. But the old stereotype of England as the peaceable kingdom and America as the violent, cowboy republic no longer holds. By 1995, with the exception of murder and rape, England's rate for every type of violent crime had far surpassed America's. The American murder rate has been substantially higher than the English rate for at least 200 years, during most of which neither country had stringent restrictions on firearms. But the English and American rates are now converging. While Americans have enjoyed over a decade of sharply declining homicide rates, rates described by the Boston Globe in 1999 as "in startling free-fall," English rates have risen dramatically. In 1981 the US rate was 8.7 times the English rate; in 1995 it was 5.7 times the English rate, and in 2002 3.5 times the English rate.

II. CRACKING DOWN ON THE LAW-ABIDING

None of this was supposed to happen in Britain where for the better part of a century, British governments have pursued a strategy for domestic safety that a 1992 Economist article characterized as requiring "a restraint on personal liberty that seems, in most civilized countries, essential to the happiness of others," a policy the magazine found at odds with "America's Vigilante Values." The safety of the British people has been staked on the thesis that fewer private guns means less crime, that any weapons in the hands of men and women, however law-abiding, pose a danger to society, and that disarming them lessens the chance that criminals will get or use weapons. In the name of public safety, the government first limited the right to private firearms, then forbade the carrying of any item useful for self-defense, and finally limited the permissible scope of self-defense itself.

The fact is England's strict firearms laws were never responsible for a low level of violent crime. The level of violent and armed crime was extraordinarily low before gun controls were introduced in 1920. A centuries-long decline in interpersonal violence ended abruptly in 1953-1954 and violent crime has been generally increasing ever since despite increasingly strict gun regulations. Historians agree that from the late middle ages to 1954, nearly five centuries, interpersonal crime in England was declining. Lawrence Stone estimated that "the homicide rates in thirteenth-century England were about twice as high as those in the sixteenth and seventeenth centuries and that those of the sixteenth and seventeenth centuries were some five to ten times higher than those today."

The decline occurred despite the introduction and increasing popularity of firearms from the sixteenth century onward, the 1689 English Bill of Rights guarantee that Protestants could have "arms for their defence," nineteenth-century judicial opinions affirming the right of every Englishman to be armed, the lack—until the 1830s—of a professional police force, and the complete absence of controls on the ownership of firearms.

By the mid-nineteenth century armed crime was almost non-existent. Between 1878 and 1886 the average number of burglaries in London in which firearms were used was two per year; from 1887 to 1891 it rose to 3.6 cases a year. A government study of handgun homicides for the years 1890-1892 found an average of one a year in a population of 30 million.

It was fear of revolution, not crime, that resulted in the first serious gun controls. In 1920 the government faced massive labor disruption, feared a Bolshevik revolution, and worried about the return of thousands of soldiers traumatized by an especially brutal war. The Firearms Act required a would-be rifle or handgun owner to obtain a certificate from the local chief of police, who was charged with determining whether the applicant had a good reason for possessing a firearm and was fit to have one. Parliament was assured that the sole intention was to keep weapons out of the hands of criminals and other dangerous persons.

 From the start, the law was applied far more broadly. Restrictive applications increased over time, thanks to Home Office instructions to police—classified until 1989—that periodically narrowed the definition of "good reason." At the outset, police were instructed that however fit the person who requested a certificate for a handgun to be used for protection, it should only be granted if he "lives in a solitary house, where protection against thieves and burglars is essential, or has been exposed to definite threats to life on account of his performance of some public duty." By 1937 police were advised to discourage applications to possess any firearm for house or personal protection. In 1964 they were informed "it should hardly ever be necessary to anyone to possess a firearm for the protection of his house or person" and that "this principle should hold good even in the case of banks and firms who desire to protect valuables or large quantities of money." In 1969 police were told "it should never be necessary for anyone to possess a firearm for the protection of his house or person."

There was no public debate or consultation at any stage about this Home Office policy which thwarted the original intent of the Firearms Act and effectively denied the right of Englishmen to "have arms for their defence." According to the Home Office, the only acceptable reason for having firearms was gun sports, and sports are not constitutionally protected.

In addition to narrowing the criteria for a certificate over the years, a series of modifications were made to the basic 1920 Firearms Act. And so we have the Firearms Acts of 1934, of 1936, of 1937, of 1965, of 1968, of 1988, and the two acts of 1997 which banned handguns. Additional gun controls were incorporated within broad criminal justice acts. Some acts allowed government to ratchet down the number of firearms in private hands; other acts were an opportunistic response to shooting incidents, and these acts were often in lieu of meaningful action that would have enhanced public safety. Nearly all the acts concentrated on limiting the access of law-abiding citizens to weapons, rather than reducing the pool of illegal firearms, or otherwise deterring violent crime.

The shotgun certificate program incorporated into the Firearms Act of 1968 is an example of opportunistic firearms legislation that had little to do with preventing crime. The notion of bringing shotguns within the certificate system had been considered for some time. When Home Secretary Sir Frank Soskice studied the matter in 1965, he decided requiring certificates for the 500,000 to as many as three million shotguns in legitimate use would burden the police and "not be justified by the benefits which would result." Roy Jenkins, who replaced him at the Home Office, came to the same conclusion. Then on August 12, 1966, three London policemen were shot dead and Britain's greatest manhunt was on. The murder weapons were handguns, not shotguns. The public demanded the reinstatement of capital punishment, which the government had abolished provisionally the previous November. Instead, Jenkins announced plans "to end the unrestricted purchase of shotguns" claiming the "criminal use of shotguns" was increasing rapidly, still more rapidly than that of other weapons." If Jenkins' motive was to divert attention from reinstatement of capital punishment he succeeded, but as authors R.A.I. Munday and J.A. Stevenson reckon it was "at the cost of approximately half a million man hours of police time per year over the ensuing twenty years, and far more than that since 1988."

Shotguns were again the target in 1988 after former paratrooper Michael Ryan went on a shooting spree in the town of Hungerford. Before an unarmed police force and an unarmed public were able to stop him, he had killed sixteen people and wounded another fourteen. In response, the Labour government introduced a firearms bill to place shotguns, the last type of firearm that could be purchased with a simple show of fitness, under controls similar to those on pistols and rifles. Shotguns were to be registered and the police could demand costly security arrangements before granting a certificate. The result was massive non-compliance. Of the 300,000 pump-action and self-loading shotguns had been sold in the years prior to the 1988 act, at most only 50,000 were submitted to proof with restricted magazines, handed in to police, or obtained certificates. A quarter of a million shotguns simply disappeared.

The handgun ban of 1997, the response to the terrible shooting of children and teachers in Dunblane, Scotland, is another example of misdirected efforts. Thomas Hamilton, the perpetrator, had a certificate for his weapons, although the shooting community repeatedly warned the local police Hamilton was not a fit person to have them. The police carried out seven investigations on Hamilton, but failed to remove his firearm certificate. In urging a handgun ban, the Labour party insisted that the number of crimes involving legal firearms was "unacceptably high" although at the time only 9 percent of English homicides were caused by firearms, of which just 14 percent of the weapons involved had ever been legally held.

Before Dunblane the number of licensed guns involved in crime in Scotland was even lower. Of the 669 homicides between 1990 and 1995 only 44 were committed with firearms, and of these only 3, or .4%, involved licensed firearms. Nonetheless public pressure, spurred by a campaign led by parents of the Dunblane victims, called for and got a complete ban on handguns.

III. CREATING A MONOPOLY OF FORCE

Forbidding the use of firearms for self-defense has merely formed a part of government policy to reserve to itself a monopoly on the use of force. In 1953 the government went beyond disarming the public of firearms and with the Prevention of Crime Act forbade individuals carrying any article in a public place "made, adapted, or intended" for an offensive purpose "without lawful authority or excuse." Carrying anything to protect oneself was branded antisocial. Any item carried for possible defense was defined as an offensive weapon. Police were given extensive power to stop and search everyone and individuals found with offensive items were guilty until proven innocent. The government claimed the prohibition was necessary to combat rising crime, although just two weeks earlier that same government had defeated an effort to reinstate corporal punishment for some types of violent crimes by insisting that crime rates were declining. Ministers disregarded an MP's plea that

> while society ought to undertake the defence of its law-abiding members, neverthe-
> less one has to remember that there are many places where society cannot get, or
> cannot get there in time. On those occasions a man has to defend himself and those
> whom he is escorting. It is not very much consolation that society will come forward
> a great deal later, pick up the bits, and punish the violent offender…A Bill of this kind,
> which is for the prevention of crime, ought not to strike at people doing nothing but
> taking reasonable precautions for the defence of themselves and those whom it is
> their natural duty to protect.

In the House of Lords, Lord Saltoun noted that "The object of a weapon was to assist weakness to cope with strength and it was this ability that the bill was framed to destroy. I do not think," he pointed out, "any government has the right—though they may very well have the power—to deprive people for whom they are responsible of the right to defend themselves." Saltoun warned that "unless there is not only a right, but also a fundamental willingness amongst the people to defend themselves, no police force, however large, can do it."

Public safety and self-defense were eroded still further by the Criminal Justice Act of 1967. In this statute the British government changed the longstanding rules for the use of force in self-defense making everything depend on what seems reasonable use of force, considered after the fact. In Textbook on Criminal Law, Glanville Williams argues that the requirement that an individual's efforts to defend himself be "reasonable" was "now stated in such mitigated terms as to cast doubt on whether it still forms part of the law." In addition to altering the common law position on self-defense, the customary responsibility to assist someone in distress was reversed: If you see an individual being attacked you are advised to "walk on by" and let the professionals handle it. A passive and dependent public seems a higher government priority than personal safety.

In contrast to the harsh attitude toward law-abiding people anxious to protect themselves and their families, the British government has taken a very solicitous attitude toward criminal predators. Most offenders are punished with community service rather than prison, even after repeated offences. The few who are incarcerated receive shorter terms than in the past, and usually serve only half of these. Community service and short prison terms save money.

To discourage self-help on the part of victims, offenders who are harmed by their victims have been able to sue them in the courts. In the recent case of Tony Martin, a Norfolk farmer who shot two burglars who broke into his home, killing one, the wounded burglar was released after serving half of his three-year sentence. He then claimed that the injury to his leg prevented him from working and interfered with his martial arts practice and his sex life. He was awarded public funds to finance his law suit against Martin. At the same time Martin, his sentence of life imprisonment reduced to five years on appeal, was denied parole because he posed a danger to burglars.

A large police force is also expensive. Hence surveillance cameras have been installed as a cheap substitute for officers on patrol. England now has more surveillance cameras than any other country. Police departments have been consolidated to save funds, leaving 70 percent of rural communities with no police presence and their residents practically unable to defend themselves. Financial considerations have trumped considerations about public safety.

The British government has removed proven deterrents to crime: a public able to defend itself, and sure punishment for violating the law. In the face of the recent wave of gun crime and violent crime, the current government's response has been to tighten gun restrictions yet again, to consider outlawing replica or toy guns, and to remove ancient legal protections for defendants such as the right of jury trials, the prohibition on double jeopardy, and restrictions on hearsay evidence.

Honest people have been disarmed, severely limited in their legal ability to defend themselves and left at the mercy of thugs. When there were no gun controls, England had an astonishingly low level of armed crime. Eighty years of increasingly stringent gun regulations, the strictest of any democracy, have failed to stop, or even to slow, the rise in gun crime. And gun crime is part of a disastrous rise in violent crime generally.

Admittedly, it is far more difficult to control illegal weapons than to impose controls on the peaceful public, far more difficult to confront the real challenges to public safety than to pass another measure designed to give government a tighter monopoly on the use of force, a monopoly it can only impose on the law-abiding. It is the honest citizens who are doubly losers: they are not permitted to protect themselves, and society has failed to protect them. William Blackstone, England's famous eighteenth-century jurist, reminded readers that the principal aim of society "is to protect individuals in the enjoyment of those absolute rights, which were vested in them by the immutable laws of nature." He defined those absolute rights, those "great and primary" rights, as personal security, personal liberty and private property. The very first of these is personal security. There was wisdom in the common law approach to public safety and self-defense that modern governments have ignored to the peril of the people they represent.

ENDNOTES

1. Home Office press notice (November 3, 1997).

2. This statement was in reference to the restrictions passed in 1987 in the wake of the so-called Hungerford massacre. Douglas Hurd, secretary of state for the Home Office, in Hansard, Parliamentary Debates (October 26, 1987), vol. 121: 59, 50, 55, 46.

3. All crime statistics are for England and Wales, not for Great Britain. The U.K. has always separated England/Wales crime statistics from Scotland and Northern Ireland. Handgun crime rises by 46 per cent (January 9, 2003), www.timesonline.co.uk.

4. Police 'winning London gun crime battle', BBC NEWS online (February 16, 2003); *Sunday Times* (January 5, 2003), at 12; "Handgun crime rises by 46 per cent" (January 9, 2003), <www.timesonline.co.uk>.

5. Helen Carter, "Liverpool football player shot in bar: Weekend attacks 'show gun crime out of control,'" Guardian (October 6, 2003).

6. "Gun crime growing 'like cancer'", BBC newsonline, May 21, 2003.

7. John Steele, "Britain the most violent country in western Europe," *The Telegraph* (October 23, 2003).

8. Sophie Goodchild, Britain is now the crime capital of the West, *Independent on Sunday* (July 14, 2002), at 1.

9. Helen Carter, "Liverpool football player shot in bar: Weekend attacks 'show gun crime out of control'", Guardian (October 6, 2003).

10. Patrick A. Langan & David P. Farrington, *Crime and Justice in the United States and in England and Wales, 1981-96*

(Bureau of Justice Statistics, U.S. Department of Justice, 1998), at iii-iv.

11. Eric H. Monkkonen, *Murder in New York City* (2001), at 178-79.

12. As measured by police statistics in 1981 the U.S. murder rate was 8.7 times England's. In 1996 it was 5.7 times England's and the figures for 2002 place it at 3.5 times the English rate. Langan & Farrington, supra note 10, at iii; Gary Mauser, *National Experiences with Firearms Regulation: Evaluating the Implications for Public Safety*, fig. 1, paper presented at Symposium on The Legal, Economic and Human Rights Implications of Civilian Firearms Ownership and Regulation (London: May 2, 2003).

13. Lawrence Stone, I*nterpersonal Violence in English Society,* 1300-1980, 29 Past and Present 101 (1983). Also see Joyce Lee Malcolm, *Guns and Violence: The English Experience* (2002), at 19-20.

14. For a discussion of legal opinions on the right of Englishmen to be armed see Joyce Lee Malcolm, *To Keep and Bear Arms: The Origins of an Anglo-American Right* (1994), at 130, 134, 167-168.

15. I am indebted to Colin Greenwood, author of *Firearms Control: A Study Of Armed Crime and Firearms Control in England and Wales* (1972) for these figures.

16. Returns giving Particulars of Cases treated for Revolver or Pistol wounds in Hospitals during the Years 1890, 1891 and 1892 (August 14, 1893) 11 Home Office, 557 of 1893-94 session at 73.

17. For a discussion of the passage of this act see Malcolm, *To Keep and Bear Arms,* supra note 13, at 170-176.

18. Guidance from Home Office on Firearms Act, 1920 (October 5, 1920), at 3.

19. Memorandum for the Guidance of the Police (Home Office: 1937).

20. Memorandum for the Guidance of the Police (Home Office: 1964), at 7.

21. Memorandum for the Guidance of the Police (Home Office: 1969), at 22.

22. See Malcolm, *Guns and Violence*, supra note 13, at 172-173.

23. *Id.* at 197-199.

24. Jenkins, quoted in *Daily Telegraph* (September 13, 1966). While it was claimed that shotgun offences had trebled since 1961, the figures were collected on a different basis every year since that date, and, as they included all "indictable offences involving shotguns" counted every sort of crime from armed robbery and poaching to the theft of old weapons. An antique weapon that was stolen was listed as a gun involved in crime. See Greenwood, *Firearms Control*, supra note 15, at chap. 8.

25. R.A.I. Munday & J.A. Stevenson, eds., *Guns & Violence: The Debate before Lord Cullen* (1996), at 166.

26. See Malcolm, *Guns and Violence*, supra note 9 at 201-202.

27. *Id* at 206-207.

28. See Munday & Stevenson, *Guns & Violence, supra* note 25, at 33, 322-23, and table I.

29. Lord Stoddard of Swindon, 582 Parl. Deb., House of Lords (October 27, 1997), at 944.

30. See Malcolm, *Guns and Violence,* supra note 13, at 203-206.

31. *Id.,* at 173-74.

32. For further information on the 1953 Prevention of Crime Act see Malcolm, *Guns and Violence, supra* note.

33. Cited by Malcolm, *Guns and Violence, supra* note 13, at 179.

34. Glanville Williams, *Textbook of Criminal Law* (2nd ed. 1983), at 507.

35. See Malcolm, *Guns and Violence*, supra note 13, at 189-93.

36. See Burglar sues farmer (December 23, 2003), news.bbc.co.uk; Stephen Wright, *Burglar's legal aid to sue* Tony Martin, Daily Mail (July 6, 2002); Malcolm, Guns and Violence, supra note 13, at 213-15.

SHOOTING SPORTS IN THE EUROPEAN UNION

DISCUSSION OF HUNTING AND FIREARMS POSSESSION

FEDERATION OF ASSOCIATION FOR HUNTING AND CONSERVATION OF THE EU

THE EUROPEAN PARLIAMENT

The democratically-elected European Parliament (EP) has over the years increased its power and influence in the EU law-making process, as most legislation proposed by the European Commission needs to be adopted jointly by the EP and the Council of Ministers under the co-decision procedure. FACE is very well aware of this key role of the EP and considers regular contacts with Members of the European Parliament (MEPs) as essential for fulfilling its tasks.

With the accession of Bulgaria and Romania to the EU in January 2007, there are a total of 785 MEPs from 27 EU Member States.

One of the most important issues dealt with by the EP during the 2007 Parliamentary year is the amendment of the 1991 "Firearms" Directive, under the co-decision procedure. FACE has established and maintained regular and useful contacts with a wide range of relevant MEPs from different Political Groups and Member States, including, of course, the Rapporteurs, Shadow Rapporteurs as well as EP officials throughout this debate on firearms.[1]

In October 2006, after a long debate, the EP adopted a Resolution on the European Commission's Action Plan on the Protection and Welfare of Animals 2006-2010. The Commission, in this document, has clearly focused on farm and research animals but suggested that the EU also has a competence in the area of welfare of wild animals.

In its final Resolution, the EP "calls on the Commission and the Member States, within the scope of their respective areas of competence, further to develop animal protection and to take full account of the protection and welfare of all animals."FACE believes that the EP could have sent a clearer message to the Commission underlining the limits of the EU competence in the field of animal welfare. Nevertheless, the vague reference to "all animals" (unlike explicit references to "wild animals" in previous EP drafts) of competence" is part of the input by FACE during all stages of discussion and its contacts with the Rapporteur (German Christian-Democrat Elisabeth Jeggle) and other key MEPs.

The EP also adopted a Resolution in May 2007 on the Commission's Communication "Halting the loss of biodiversity by 2010 - and beyond - Sustaining ecosystem services for human well-being." The Resolution considers that the NATURA 2000 Network must be strengthened to safeguard and restore wild species, and biodiversity considerations need to be further integrated into agriculture and fisheries policies, as well as into spatial planning at national, regional and local levels. It further urges a Community response to the threat posed by the introduction of invasive alien species - the second most important threat, after the after the destruction of habitats, to biodiversity. The Resolution also calls on better co-operation and stronger partnerships between key stakeholder-groups, such as landowners, wildlife-users and conservation groups, supporting "... in particular partnerships with hunters, the fishing community, farmers and foresters..." The Draft Resolution mentioned "hunting" as a possible threat to biodiversity but FACE was able to clarify – thanks to the support of the Rapporteur, Cypriote Communist Adamos Adamous, and of the Shadow Rapporteur for the Christian-Democrat EPP-ED Group, Irish MEP Avril Doyle – that this threat applies only to "unsustainable hunting".

European Parliament in Strasbourg, France

The need to be permanently alert was illustrated by two unhelpful Resolutions adopted by the EP using an obscure provision of its Rules of Procedure that allows, further to a question for an oral answer, such adoption with virtually no previous debate. In March 2007, the EP adopted a Resolution about "illegal" spring hunting in Malta and in May a second one, completely opposed to sustainable wildlife use, concerning the Conference of the Parties (CoP14) to the Convention on International Trade in Endangered Species (CITES). FACE and its allies at the EP need to draw lessons from this kind of initiatives orchestrated by animals' rights groups, which undermine the credibility of this democratic institution insofar as highly technical topics are addressed in a superficial way.

THE INTERGROUP "SUSTAINABLE HUNTING, BIODIVERSITY & COUNTRYSIDE ACTIVITIES"

The Intergroup *"Sustainable Hunting, Biodiversity & Countryside Activities"* in the European Parliament has been provided consultation by FACE since it was set up back in 1985 and usually has roughly 80 Members. They consist of MEPs from nearly all Political Groups[2] and EU Member States, making this Intergroup (IG) one of the largest and most active ones in the EP. Regularly new members join the IG, very often from the new Member States.

In 2006-2007, the IG met six times in Strasbourg, France to discuss a wide-range of relevant topics, with active participation from key MEPs from all Political Groups as well as experts from other European and national institutions and related organizations.

In September 2006 the IG dealt with the "Firearms" Proposal, for which MEPs advocated a rational debate to avoid unjustified restrictions to the legitimate use of sporting firearms. The November 2006 meeting gave MEPs an opportunity to exchange views on the future of hunting in society. In February 2007, MEPs were informed about the implementation of the "Game meat" Regulations, as well as, the drafting of new "Animal-by products" Regulation, scheduled to be submitted to the EP by the end of the year. During a joint meeting in March 2007 with the "Sustainable Development" Intergroup, a high level delegation from Namibia, led by its *Minister of the Environment*, Hon. Willem Konjore, was welcomed to address the role of sustainable use of wildlife in relation to the forthcoming *Conference of the Parties* of the CITES Convention (Convention on International Trade in Endangered Species of Wild Fauna and Flora). The outcome of this very interesting debate was the unanimous adoption of a *Joint Declaration*, calling upon the EU to recognize the contribution of sustainable trade in CITES-listed species for rural development and wildlife conservation. The topic of the May 2007 meeting was the impact of cormorants on biodiversity in Europe. MEPs adopted a *Declaration* acknowledging the significant damage caused by cormorant on wild fish stocks and on biodiversity at large, stressing the need for a European management strategy as well as precise *Guidelines* for applying Article 9 "Derogations" of the 1979 "*Birds*" Directive. At the June 2007 IG meeting, MEPs examined how to assess the sustainability of hunting. Based on a number of objective criteria and measurable indicators, the different hunting-related aspects can be evaluated in an open and transparent process, involving hunters as well as other relevant stakeholders.

The rare Balkan Chamois

IS THE EU COMPETENT TO DEAL WITH THE WELFARE OF WILD ANIMALS?

The first mention to animal welfare in the European Treaties was made in *Declaration No 24 on the protection of animals*, annexed to the 1992 Final Act of the EU Treaty - The Maastricht Treaty). This was completed by the *Protocol on protection and welfare of animals*, annexed to the 1997 Amsterdam Treaty[3], which considers animals as "*sentient beings*" and indicates that "*In formulating and implementing the Community's agriculture, transport, internal market and research policies, the Community and the Member States shall pay full regard to the welfare requirements of animals*".

The Protocol indicates, however, that this concern had to respect "*the legislative or administrative provisions and customs of the Member States relating in particular to religious rites, cultural traditions and regional heritage*".

This means that the EU is competent to adopt legislation on welfare of animals only within the framework and the aims of the agriculture, transport, internal market and research policies - environment and biodiversity are **not** mentioned. And animal welfare is not an end in itself, but only a factor that must be fully taken into account when formulating and implementing these policies. The EC Treaty therefore provides no legal basis for the introduction of legislation specifically intended to improve the welfare of animals.

Concern for the welfare of domestic (farm) animals is based on the consideration that better living standards for these animals will result in better animal health and therefore in better animal products. Another argument - most important from a legal point of view – is that the EU needs to set common (minimum) welfare standards in order to avoid distortions of competition that would result if the requirements imposed on farmers diverged greatly from one Member State to another.

Even before the above mentioned *Protocol* to the EC Treaty, several legal instruments had been adopted as part of the Common Agriculture and Common Market Policies. Decision 78/923/EEC[4], which approved on behalf of the European Economic Community (EEC, predecessor of the EU) the *European Convention on the Protection of Animals Kept for Farming Purposes* (adopted two years earlier by another international organization, the Council of Europe) stated that "the protection of animals is not in itself one of the objectives of the Community (…) however, …. *disparities between existing national laws on the protection of animals kept for farming purposes … may give rise to unequal conditions of competition and … consequently have an indirect effect on the proper functioning of the common market* (…)."

Other examples are the 1986 Directive[5] on the protection of laying hens using the Article of the Treaty on the Common Agricultural Policy as legal basis, and another 1986 Directive regarding the protection of animals used for experimental and other scientific purposes[6] based on the EC Treaty provisions on the Internal Market.

Red fox © Malene Thyssen

The Court of Justice of the European Communities has confirmed[7] that "*ensuring the welfare of animals does not form part of the objectives of the Treaty*" and that there is "*no indication that the need to ensure animal welfare is to be regarded as a general principle of Community law.*"

Since 1979, the EU has adopted a number of legal instruments (such as the "Birds" Directive[8] and "Habitats" Directive[9] dealing with the conservation of wild species – but not with the welfare of individual wild animals. According to the EC Treaty, the Environmental Policy contributes to the protection of the quality of the environment, the protection of human health, a rational use of natural resources and the promotion of environmental measures at international level. The conservation of wild animal species is clearly part of the Environmental policy, in particular to ensure that human activities do not have a negative impact on biological diversity.

The welfare of individual wild animals, however, is not linked with the conservation of the species.

Major international instruments for wildlife conservation, such as the *UN Convention on Biological Diversity* (1993) or the Council of Europe's *BERN Convention*[10] do not deal with welfare of animals. The CITES Convention, regulating international trade in wild species, addresses the living conditions of *captive* wild specimen, but only to ensure that their survival is not compromised during transport. This is also the approach of the 1997 Regulation implementing CITES at EU level[11]).

Following an orchestrated campaign against the commercial harvesting of Seal pups in Canada, a Directive[12] was adopted under Article 235 of the EEC Treaty (now 308 of the EC Treaty), which provides for action in a domain not specifically listed in the Treaty, provided that all Member States agree. As this procedure still requires that the reasons on which an act is based is stated, the EEC justified it by referring to the concern on the conservation status of Hooded seal populations – not on animal welfare grounds.

This also applied to the 1991 Regulation banning leg-hold traps[13]**),** not because they would be "cruel" (and the term "welfare" was nowhere mentioned in the text) but because such traps would be unselective. Its legal base was Article 130s (now 175, Environmental policy) - because the *BERN Convention "prohibits for certain species, the use of all indiscriminate means of capture and killing including traps, if the latter are applied for large-scale or non-selective capture or killing"*, combined with Article 113 of the EC Treaty[14] (now 133, Commercial policy)– *"in order ... to avoid distortion of competition, it is necessary to ensure that external trade measures relating to them are uniformly applied throughout the Community."*

Likewise, the 1999 Directive relating to the keeping of wild animals in zoos[15] nowhere refers to the concept of "welfare"; its justification is the need *"for the adoption of measures by Member States for the licensing and inspection of zoos in the Community, thereby strengthening the role of zoos in the conservation of biodiversity."* That is why the Directive only lays down minimal conditions to satisfy the biological and conservation requirements of (captive) wild animals.

In the past, the European Commission has acknowledged – in particular in its answers to *Written Questions*[16] from MEPs - that the EU competence on animal welfare is limited to the agriculture, transport, internal market and research policies. The Commission explicitly ruled out any EU competence on animal welfare in relation to, for instance, greyhound racing, bullfighting, rodeos or stray animals.

This position seems to have changed a first time with the Proposal for a Directive on humane trapping standards[17], intended to implement in the EU the *Agreement on international humane trapping standards* (AIHTS**),** concluded in 1998 with Canada and the Russian Federation and an Agreed minute with the USA. It based its Proposal – which contained only very indirect references to wildlife conservation or the environment - on Article 175 of the EC Treaty (Environmental Policy), although the EU has no competence to legislate on *welfare of wild* animals on the basis of this Article. The Commission's Proposal was, however, rejected in November 2005 by an overwhelming majority of MEPs, be it for very different reasons. The *Rapporteur*, Austrian Socialist Karin SCHEELE, supported by her Group and the Greens, advocated the rejection of the Proposal for considering it not enough stringent and not based on the latest scientific data. Other Political Groups, in particular the IND/DEM and the EPP-ED (including members of the Committee on Legal Affairs), clearly supported the rejection of the Proposal because of the incorrect choice of the legal basis.

More recently, the Commission presented in January 2006 its Communication for an Action Plan on Animal Welfare 2006-2010[18], according to which *"animal welfare is not only related to the production of food and important challenges exist with regard to protecting the welfare of experimental, zoo and companion animals etc. The importance attached to animal welfare is evolving in terms of ethical concerns and this has become a "cultural attitude" for European society"* and that consequently *"the Community should also actively identify trans-boundary problems in the area of animal welfare, relating to companion or farm animals, wildlife, etc".* The Commission further makes an amalgam of animal welfare and

Great Bustard

wildlife conservation and assumes that Article 175 of the EC Treaty covers both domains – which is not the case. It also includes in the list of existing EU legislation on the protection and welfare of animals the "Zoo" Directive, the "Leghold Trap" Regulation, the "CITES" Regulation, the "Seal Pups" Directive, the "Birds" Directive and the "Habitats" Directive – which is also incorrect.

The Commission's statement that *"To date the formulation of legislative initiatives has been one of the main tools used at Community level to ensure that animals do not endure avoidable pain, distress or suffering and obliging the owner/keeper/hunter/trader or any other persons dealing with animals to respect minimum welfare requirements"* is misleading, to say the least. There is not, for the moment, any EU provision on how an *owner* must treat an animal not kept for farming purposes, such as a pet or a companion animal, nor on how a *hunter* should deal with the welfare of *wild* animals.

FIREARMS DIRECTIVE

Over the last two decades, FACE has been closely involved in the drafting, adoption and implementation of the 1991 "Firearms" Directive[19]. Aimed to facilitate the free movement of persons and goods in the Internal Market, as an accompanying measure to the abolition (or at least relaxing) of internal frontier controls between EU Member States, this Directive lays down a *minimum* level of harmonization of rules for the acquisition and possession of firearms according to four categories of firearms (A-B-C-D)[20], with Member States entitled to take more stringent measures. It further lays

Semi- natural habitat wetland

down conditions for the transfer of firearms between Member States and introduced - as a result of an idea launched initially by FACE and strongly supported by the *Rapporteur* at the time, German Christian-Democrat MEP Karl von Wogau - the *European Firearms Pass* facilitating legal holders of firearms (in particular hunters) to travel with them throughout the territory of the EU.

In March 2006, the European Commission tabled a Proposal to amend the Directive in order to implement, in the EU, the United Nations *Protocol against the Illicit Manufacturing of and Trafficking in Firearms, their Parts and Components and Ammunitions*[21]. The Proposal, which is well-balanced, merely intends to introduce some technical changes in the Directive in the light of the UN Protocol, without modifying the conditions for the acquisition and possession of firearms.

The first EU body to express its view on the Commission's Proposal was the European Economic and Social Committee (EESC), which adopted a non-binding *Opinion* in September 2006. Representatives from FACE and IEACS (European manufacturers of hunting and sporting firearms) participated as experts in the discussions at the EESC and gave some advice to the *Rapporteur*, Portuguese José Pegado Liz: this input was reflected in the final Opinion. Under the *co-decision* procedure, the EP has examined the Proposal and FACE was once more closely involved in the parliamentary process.

The EP Committee on the Internal Market and Consumer Protection (IMCO), as responsible one for this dossier, appointed in 2006 German Green MEP Gisela Kallenbach as *Rapporteur*. Her insistence to organize a mini-hearing on firearms (held at the EP in October 2006) for an amendment that was supposed to be purely technical already indicated a tendency to overplay the "risks" of private ownership of firearms. The *Draft Report* that she presented in November 2006 came nevertheless as an unpleasant surprise to FACE, as it intended to make the 1991 Directive considerably more restrictive, proposing, among other things: to abolish categories C and D so that all hunting & sporting firearms (and ammunition) would become subject to an individual *authorization* procedure, including for holders of a valid hunting permit or a sport-shooting license; to introduce a minimum age of 18 for the possession **any** firearm, without any possibility of a derogation for hunting and sport-shooting; to impose a 15-working day "cooling off" period for the acquisition of **any** firearm, even for law-abiding persons already possessing one; to forbid the legal acquisition of firearms through means of distance communication (mail order); other amendments rendering legal manufacturing of and legal trade in civil firearms extremely difficult – having thus an impact not only on the professional sector but also on the final consumer.

On its side, the EP Committee on Civil Liberties, Justice and Home Affairs (LIBE) also decided to prepare an *Opinion* and appointed shortly afterwards German Liberal MEP Alexander Alvaro as *Draftsperson*. His proposed amendments to the text of the Directive were considerably less restrictive than those of Mrs. Kallenbach, but he also intended to change the classification of firearms so that all of them become subject to *authorization*.

In coordination with the European organizations representing manufacturers (AFEMS for sporting ammunition and IEACS for sporting firearms), dealers (AECAC), sportshooting (ESC) and collectors (FESAC), FACE has been particularly active in explaining in a reasoned way to MEPs from all Political Groups that these restrictions are unjustified and would not contribute in any way to prevent or reduce crime, which is linked to illegal firearms.. *MEP (EPP-ED; France)*

Shotguns

Those same restrictions would have, on the other hand, a very negative impact on persons legally involved with firearms, such as hunters and sportshooters (over 7 million EU citizens), dealers and manufacturers (mainly small and medium-sized enterprises). This contribution to the EP debate has indeed proved useful.

The EP LIBE Committee adopted on 11th June 2007 an *Opinion* that requires the granting of "*a license or a permit in accordance with national legislation*" for the acquisition and possession of all firearms, as well as linking every firearm to its current owner. This approach was part of the compromise reached in this Committee not to change the current classification of firearms in the Directive. Furthermore, the *Opinion* of the LIBE Committee considers that *European Firearms Pass* must be regarded as the only document necessary for hunters (and sport-shooters) to travel with their firearms to another EU Member State.

The EP IMCO adopted on 27th June a *Report* that confirmed the abovementioned amendments of the LIBE Committee (i.e. maintaining all four categories of firearms and giving significantly more weight to the *European Firearms Pass*). In addition to this, the *Report* considers that the minimum age of 18 for possessing a firearm should not apply to young hunters accompanied by an adult hunter, the idea of a 15-working day "cooling off" period before acquiring any firearm was abandoned, acquisition of firearms through means of distance communication is regulated but not banned and the (mainly marking) conditions for manufacturers become feasible.

On the 29th November, 2007, the Plenary Session of the EP adopted by an overwhelming majority (588 against 14) the final text for the new Directive (jointly with the Council of Ministers), ending this complex procedure that started in March 2006. At the time of writing, its final preparation for publication in the *Official Journal* of the EU is expected in the coming weeks but a first analysis of the situation can already be made.

Indeed, the 1991 classification of firearms (and their ammunition) into 4 categories was *de facto* maintained, despite attempts by the Parliament's main *Rapporteur*, German *Green* MEP Gisela KALLENBACH to have <u>all</u> sporting firearms classified as either *forbidden* or else subject to strict *authorisation*. Registration will only become required for category D firearms (= single-shot shotguns) "*placed on the market"* (not for those already possessed), including, from 2010 onwards, measures enabling linkage to their owner. To that end, dealers will have to keep a register and Member States (as from 2014) a "computerised data filing system" in which firearms shall be recorded.

The "new" Directive further explicitly indicates that persons acquiring or possessing *any* firearm should not be likely to represent a *"danger to themselves, to public order or to public safety"* - a reasonable requirement that FACE, of course, fully agrees with.

The original intention of the *Rapporteur* to delete the existing exception for people under the age of 18 to acquire and possess (i.e. use) a firearm *"for hunting or target shooting"* was adapted, insofar that in the future, minors will only be prohibited to *purchase* firearms but they should keep the possibility to acquire them by other means (gift, inheritance, etc) and to use them for hunting or sport shooting when they *have parental permission or are under parental guidance or guidance of an adult with a valid firearms or hunting license or are within a licensed training or otherwise approved centre*. Considering the controversial nature of this issue and a tragic incident in Finland (where an 18 year-old registered sport-shooter killed 8 people) only a few weeks before the final vote in Parliament, this is the best that could be achieved.

Due to the objection of certain Member States (in particular the UK), it has however not been possible to obtain sufficient support for a positive proposal by the *Rapporteur*, namely to delete the possibility for Member States to impose on visiting hunters and sport-shooters an additional "import" permit next to the *European Firearms Pass*. The possibility for national authorities to make the acceptance of the *Pass* *"conditional upon the payment of any fee or charge"* has nevertheless been abolished.

Steelshot Shotgun Shells

Other positive elements were *inter alia* the defeat of various negative proposals, such as the explicit reference to "... *the risks of violent deaths and injuries due to small arms"* or the introduction of a 15-day "cooling-off" prior to the acquisition of any firearm. The proposal to *prohibit* acquisition of firearms through means of distance communication (e.g. internet or mail order) was watered down into *"strictly controlled"*. The marking requirements for manufacturers of civil firearms and ammunition will be reasonable (with the possibility for Member States to use the CIP proof-house system) and authorised dealers will not see their capacity to transfer firearms between Member States hindered.

The overall outcome is, considering the original Proposal and various amendments tabled in the Parliament, satisfactory and the amended Directive will have little or no impact on hunters and sport-shooters in the EU. FACE closely cooperated with the other sectors concerned and succeeded in obtaining good result on all essential issues.

FACE has continues its efforts to convince the EU to give more explicit recognition to the Guidance Document on Hunting that was published in August 2004 by the European Commission (available in all EU languages under: http://ec.europa.eu/environment/nature/nature_conservation/focus_wild_birds/sustainable_hunting/index_en.htm). This interpretative guide is a key element of the *Agreement* reached in October 2004 between FACE and *BirdLife International*, in so far that it clarifies, in combination with the Commissions "Key-concepts" report (containing for each Member State the calendar - per decade - of reproduction and return migration periods for each of the 82 huntable bird species, listed in Annex II), the conformity of the beginning and / or the end of hunting seasons with the provisions of Article 7§4 of the Directive 79/409/EEC. Aware of the problem that national authorities, administrations and courts remain reluctant to fully take into account the *Guidance Document* as long as it has not received a more solid legal base, e.g. by being incorporated in one way or another in EU law, FACE has systematically supported initiatives to that end. Indeed, it was already at the EU Conference of November 2004 in Bergen op Zoom (Netherlands), marking the 25th anniversary of the Directive that a clear agreement had been reached by the European Commission, Member States and International NGO's to amend Annex V "Research" of this Directive and this *inter alia* by including in it a specific reference to the Commission's *Guidance Document*.

EP Hemicycle (Plenary Session)

Amending this particular Annex V only requires the agreement from (a majority of) the Committee *for the adaptation to technical and scientific progress* of the Directive - better known as the *ORNIS Committee*. For amending most other Annexes, however - as well as the text of the Directive itself - the much heavier *Co-Decision Procedure* is required, involving inter alia a formal consultation of the European Parliament.22 In 2005, FACE and *BirdLife (www.birdlife.org)* therefore jointly wrote a letter to the European Commission in support of such an amendment of Annex V and throughout 2005 and 2006, it seemed that this formal adoption by the ORNIS Committee would be a mere formality. Unfortunately, because of procedural objections from the Commission's own *Legal Service*, this option had to be abandoned.23

Since then, FACE (as well as the "Sustainable Hunting" *Intergroup* in the European Parliament and several Member States) has been in regular contact with the Services of DG Environment to convince them to take an appropriate initiative. These efforts seem to have paid off as at the ORNIS Committee meeting on 4th July 2007, the *Head of Unit* "Nature & Biodiversity" announced that the formal procedure has been launched which should lead to the adoption of a *Commission Recommendation* to the Member States to apply the Commission's *Guidance Document on Hunting under the Birds Directive* and to promote it as some kind of "Code of Best Practice." If adopted, as scheduled, after the summer, this *Recommendation* would be published (together with the text of the *Guidance Document* as sole annex) in the *Official Journal* in all 22 EU languages before the end of 2008.

FACE further continues to be involved with and to monitor very closely the drafting and possible approval of final Management Plans for huntable bird species. Already over ten years ago, the Commission and the ORNIS Committee agreed – based on data provided by *BirdLife International* – that 21 Annex II bird species could be *considered* to have an Unfavourable Conservation Status. In November 2006, the ORNIS Committee approved six *Management Plans* (for Pintail *Anas acuta*, Red-crested Pochard *Netta rufina*, Velvet Scoter *Melanitta fusca*, Curlew *Numenius arquata*, Turtle Dove *Streptopelia turtur* and Skylark *Alauda arvensis*) that are now also available on the Commission's website under: http://ec.europa.eu/environment/nature/nature_conservation/focus_wild_birds/species_birds_directive/index_en.htm.

FACE is in favour of a correct implementation of such *Management Plans* as the Commission has made it clear on more than one occasion that they have to be seen as **non-legally binding** tools to assist Member States in their efforts to restore these huntable species to a *Favourable Conservation Status* - and **not** intended to outlaw the legitimate activity of hunting.

Another new process FACE intends to participate in is the updating as well as completing with biological data from the 12 new Member States of the above mentioned "Key-concepts" document, as it is an essential tool for the correct interpretation and application of the Directive's Article 7 regarding hunting seasons.

CONCLUDING REMARKS

The amendments to the 1991 "Firearms" Directive will have to be implemented by Member States, and FACE, on behalf of all European hunters, will keep monitoring the situation and give guidance to developments in this domain.

The correct interpretation of the 1979 "Birds" Directive, in particular in relation to "pest" species (Wood pigeon, corvids, cormorants), to the dates for open seasons and to the concept of Management Plans for huntable bird species considered to be in an unfavourable conservation status (such as Woodcock) will further require considerable attention in the years to come. To a lesser degree, this also applies to the 1991 "Habitats" Directive and its provisions concerning NATURA 2000 sites and the management of large carnivores.

Another concern is the on-going revision of the "Animal by-products" Regulation, for which FACE will remain in contact with the European Commission officials in order to make sure that future rules and provisions will not adversely affect game bird rearing, shooting, stalking (trophies are animal by-products), etc. This also applies to the practical implementation of the 2006 "Food Hygiene" Regulations in relation to wild game and venison.

Last but not least, the increased attention at EU level for the welfare of wild animals (seals, fur bearing animals but also other "game" species) will require continuous monitoring of the political scene, as well as providing correct information to decision-makers.

Endnotes

1. *Rapporteur* is a person appointed by a deliberative body to investigate an issue or a situation, and report back to that body.

2. Members of the European Parliament, apart from non-attached members, generally belong to alliance/ associations called Political Groups, which draw together various national political parties based on ideology rather than national affiliation or language. 20 MEPs from at least one-fifth of the Member States are needed to form a political group.

3. Treaty of Amsterdam, Luxembourg: Office for Official Publications of the European Communities, 1997.

4. Council Decision 78/923/EEC of 19 June 1978 concerning the conclusion of the European Convention for the protection of animals kept for farming purposes; Official Journal L 120, 4/5/1978, p. 1–4.

5. Council Directive 86/113/EEC of 25 March 1986 laying down minimum standards for the protection of laying hens kept in battery cages; Official Journal L 095 , 10/04/1986 p. 45-48.

6. Council Directive 86/609/EEC of 24 November 1986 on the approximation of laws, regulations and administrative provisions of the Member States regarding the protection of animals used for experimental and other scientific purposes; Official Journal L 358 , 18/12/1986 p. 1-28.

7. Judgment of the Court of 12 July 2001 in Case C-189/01.

8. Council Directive 79/409/EEC of 2 April 1979 on conservation of wild bird; Official Journal L 103, 25/4/1979, p. 1-26.

CENSUS OF THE NUMBER OF HUNTERS IN EUROPE

Countries	km²x10³		x10⁶	%	/km²	
Albania	29	17000	3,6	0,6	124	1:176
Austria	84	115000	8,2	1,4	98	1:70
Belgium	31	20000	10,4	0,2	341	1:500
Bosnia -Herzegovina	51	50000	4,6	1,2	90	1:80
Bulgaria	111	110000	7,7	1,4	69	1:66
Croatia	57	55000	4,5	1,4	79	1:73
Cyprus	9	45000	0,8	6,4	89	1:15
Czech Republic	79	110000	10,2	1,1	129	1:91
Denmark	43	165000	5,4	3,3	125	1:327
Estonia	45	15000	1,3	1.2	29	1:87
Finland	338	305000	5,2	5,8	15	1:17
France	544	1313000	60,5	2,1	111	1:47
Germany	357	348000	82,7	0,4	231	1:237
Greece	132	270000	11,1	2,7	84	1:37
Hungary	93	54500	10,1	0,5	109	1:183
Ireland	70	350000	4,1	8,9	58	1:12

Countries	km²x10³	(hunters)	x10⁶	%	/km²	/
Italy	301	750000	58,1	1,3	193	1:77
Latvia	65	25000	2,3	1,2	35	1:80
Lithuania	65	32000	3,6	0,9	55	1:113
Luxembourg	3	2000	0,4	0,5	133	1:200
Malta	0,3	15000	0,4	3,7	1333	1:27
Moldova	34	-	4,3	-	126	-
Montenegro	14	-	0,7	-	50	-
Netherlands	42	26500	16,6	0,1	395	1:626
Norway	324	190000	4,6	4,8	14	1:21
Poland	313	106000	38,5	0,3	123	1:363
Portugal	92	230000	10,6	2,3	115	1:43
Romania	238	60000	22,3	0,3	94	1:372
Serbia	88	80000	10,1	0,7	115	1:137
Slovakia	49	55000	5,4	1,1	110	1:100
Slovenia	20	22000	2	1	100	1:91
Spain	505	980000	43,1	2,4	80	1:44
Switzerland	41	30000	7,6	0,4	185	1:233
Sweden	450	290000	9	3,2	20	1:31
Turkey	781	300000	71,2	0,4	91	1:237
United Kingdom	243	800000	59,7	1,3	248	1:74

9. Council Directive 92/43/EEC of 21 May 1992 on the conservation of natural habitats and wild fauna and flora; Official Journal L 206, 22/7/1992, p. 7-50.

10. *The Convention on the conservation of European wildlife and natural habitats, Bern, 1979.*

11. Council Regulation 338/97 of 9 December 1996 on the protection of species of wild fauna and flora by regulating trade therein; Official Journal L 298, 01/11/1997 p. 70).

12. Council Directive 83/129/EEC of 28 March 1983 concerning the importation into Member States of skins of certain seal pups and products derived therefrom; *Official Journal L 91, 9/4/1983, p. 30–31*

13. Council Regulation 3254/91/EEC of 4 November 1991 prohibiting the use of leghold traps in the Community and the introduction into the Community of pelts and manufactured goods of certain wild animal species originating in countries which catch them by means of leghold traps or trapping methods which do not meet international humane trapping standards; Official Journal L 308, 9/11/1991, p. 1–4.

14. Treaty establishing the European Community (Nice consolidated version) - Part Three: Community policies - Title IX: Common commercial policy - Article 133 - Article 113 - EC Treaty (Maastricht consolidated version) - Article 113 - EEC Treaty; Official Journal C 325, 24/12/2002 p. 90-91.

15. Council Directive 1999/22/EC of 29 March 1999 relating to the keeping of wild animals in zoos; Official Journal L 94, 9/4/1999, p. 24–26.

16. MEPs are entitled to submit oral or written questions to the Commission, the Council or the European Central Bank on any aspect of the EU's activities.

17. Directive of the European Parliament and of the Council COM(2004) 532 final –COD 2004/0183 introducing humane trapping standards for certain animal species.

18. COMMUNICATION FROM THE COMMISSION TO THE EUROPEAN PARLIAMENT AND THE COUNCIL, on a Community Action Plan on the Protection and Welfare of Animals 2006-2010; COM/2006/0013 final.

19. Council Directive 91/477/EEC of 18 June 1991 on control of the acquisition and possession of weapons; Official Journal L 256, 13/09/1991 p. 51-58.

20. For the purposes of Directive 91/477/EEC, 'firearm' means: A. Any object which falls into one of the following categories, unless it meets the definition but is excluded for one of the reasons listed in section III. A – Prohibited firearms ; B – Firearms subject to authorisation ; C – Firearms subject to declaration ; D- Other firearms.

21. untreaty.un.org/English/notpubl/18-12_c_E.doc

22. The co-decision procedure is the main legislative procedure by which law can be adopted in the European Community, the first of the three pillars of the European Union. The co-decision procedure gives the European Parliament the power to adopt legislation jointly with the Council of the European Union, requiring the two bodies to agree on an identical text before any proposal can become law.

23. The Legal Service is an internal department of the Commission reporting directly to the President of the

Commission. The role of the Legal Service is twofold: to provide legal advice to the Commission and its services, and to represent the Commission in all court cases. The provision of legal advice ensures the legality of the Commission's decisions. It is of vital importance in preventing or reducing the risk of subsequent litigation.

Members of FACE:

Albania	National Association of Hunters of Albania	
Austria	Zentralstelle Österreichischer Landesjagdverbände	www.ljv.at
Belgium	Royal Saint-Hubert Club de Belgique	
Bosnia-Herzegovina	Association of the Hunting Organisations of Bosnia & Herzegovina	
Bulgaria	Union of Hunters and Anglers of Bulgaria	www.slrb-bg.com
Croatia	Croatian Hunters'Association	www.hrvatski-lovacki-savez.hr
Cyprus	Cyprus Federation for Hunting and Wildlife Conservation	
Czech Republic	Českomoravská Myslivecká Jednota	www.cmmj.cz
Denmark	Danish Hunters' Association	www.jaegerforbundet.dk
Estonia	Estonian Hunters' Society	www.ejs.ee
Finland	Hunters' Central Organization	www.riista.fi
France	Fédération Nationale des Chasseurs	www.chasseurdefrance.com
Germany	Deutscher Jagdschutz-Verband e.v	www.jagd-online.de
Greece	Hellenic Hunters Confederation	www.ksellas.gr
Hungary	Hungarian Hunters' National Association	www.omvk.hu
Ireland	National Association of Regional Game Councils	www.nargc.ie
Italy	FACE Italia - Federazione Italiana della Caccia	www.anuu.org / www.fidc.it
Latvia	Latvian Hunters' Association	www.latma.lv
Lithuania	Lithuanian Hunters' & Fishermen Association	
Luxembourg	Fédération Saint-Hubert des Chasseurs du Grand-duché de Luxembourg	www.fshcl.lu
Malta	Federation for Hunting & Conservation – Malta	www.huntinginmalta.org.mt
Moldova	Prezidiul Societătii Vănătorilor Şi Pescarilor din Moldova – SVPM	
Montenegro	Hunting Association of Montenegro	www.lovackisayez.cg.yu
Netherlands	Koninklijke Nederlandse Jagers Vereniging – K.N.J.V.	www.knjv.nl
Norway	Norwegian Association of Hunters and Anglers	www.njff.no
Poland	Polish Hunters Association	www.pzlow.pl
Portugal	Confederação Nacional dos Caçadores Portugueses	www.cncp.pt
Romania	Association des Chasseurs et des Pêcheurs Sportifs de Roumanie	
Serbia	Lovački savez Srbije	www.lovacki-savez-srbije.com
Slovakia	Slovak Hunting Union	www.spzba.sk
Slovenia	Lovska zveza Slovenije	www.lovska-zveza.si
Spain	Real Federación Española de Caza	www.fecaza.com
Switzerland	JagdSchweiz / ChasseSuisse	www.jadgschweiz.org
Sweden	Swedish Hunters' Association	www.jagareforbundet.se
Turkey	Turkish Shooting & Hunting Federation	www.taf.gov.tr
United Kingdom	The Countryside Alliance	www.countryside-alliance.org
	British Association for Shooting and Conservation	www.base.org.uk

SOCIOLOGY

SOME INTERNATIONAL EVIDENCE ON GUN BANS AND MURDER RATES

GARY MAUSER

The Attorney General of Ontario has recently claimed that civilian ownership of firearms exacerbates or contributes to an increase in the murder rate, and because of this, he proposes banning handguns (Kari, 2007). This canard does not square, however, with international criminological research that shows that nations with more civilian firearms—even more handguns— are not more likely to suffer from higher rates of homicide than those nations with fewer firearms.

An extensive study that I recently published with American criminologist and constitutional lawyer Don Kates confirms the negative results of previous international studies (Kates and Mauser, 2007).[1] Our study compared data from a large number of nations around the world. We reanalyzed publicly available data from United Nations studies and the Small Arms Survey from Geneva to examine the link between civilian firearm ownership and homicide and suicide rates.

In Europe, for example, there were very few instances of nations with high gun ownership having higher murder rates than neighbouring nations with lower gun ownership (tables 1 and 2). If anything, the reverse tends to be the case, for reasons discussed below. For example, though Norway has one of the highest rates of firearm ownership per capita in Western Europe, it nevertheless has one of the lowest murder rates. Other nations with high firearms ownership and comparably low murder rates include Denmark, Greece, Switzerland, Germany, and Austria. Holland has a 50 percent higher murder rate than Norway despite having the lowest rate of firearm ownership in Europe. And Luxembourg, despite its total handgun ban, has a murder rate that is comparable to countries such as Norway and Austria.

In North America, the link is not so clear cut, but the comparison among Canada, Mexico, and the United States still does not support the thesis of more guns, more murder (table 3). The United States has the highest number of civilian guns per capita, but does not have the highest homicide rate. That distinction is reserved for Mexico, which has the lowest number of civilian guns. Canada has the lowest homicide rate of the three countries but has an intermediate gun density.

Bans are rarely effective. In nations where guns are less available, criminals manage to get them anyway. After decades of ever-stricter gun controls, Great Britain banned handguns and confiscated them from all permit holders in 1997. Yet from 1997 to 2005, both total homicides and gun homicides had increased by more than 25 percent.[2] Despite the confiscation of law-abiding Englishmen's handguns, a serving Metropolitan Police officer sums up the situation: "Gun crime is out of control on the streets of Britain" (UK News, 2007).

Even if gun bans did work, many alternative weapons are available to would-be murderers. Eight decades of police-state enforcement of handgun prohibition have kept Russian gun ownership low, resulting in few gun murders. Yet Russia's murder rates have long been four times higher than those in the US and 20 times higher than rates in countries such as Norway. Former Soviet nations like Lithuania also ban handguns and severely restrict other guns, yet have murder rates that are 10 to 15 times higher than in European nations with much higher gun ownership (table 2).

On a world-wide level, it is a myth that nations with more firearms in civilian hands suffer from higher homicide rates. The United Nations surveyed homicide rates and gun ownership in 33 nations (United Nations, 1997). The lack of a relationship is vividly displayed in figure 1.[3]

NATION	MURDER RATE	GUN OWNERSHIP RATE	MURDER RATE YEAR
Table 1: Gun Ownership and Murder Rates in Europe and Scandinavia (per 100,000 people)			
Russia	20.54	4,000	2002
Lithuania	11.70	0	1998
Hungary	2.22	2,000	2003
Finland	1.98	39,000	2004
Sweden	1.87	24,000	2001
Poland	1.79	1,500	2003
France	1.65	30,000	2003
Denmark	1.21	18,000	2003
Holland	1.20	300	2002
Greece	1.12	11,000	2003
Switzerland	0.99	16,000	2003
Germany	0.99	10,000	2003
Luxembourg	0.90	0	2002
Norway	0.81	36,000	2001
Austria	0.80	17,000	2002

Notes:

1. This table covers all the Continental European nations for which the two data sets given are both available. In every case we have given the homicide data for 2003 or the closest year thereto because that is the year of the publication from which the gun ownership data are taken. Sources: The homicide rates data come from the pamphlets by the Canadian Centre for Justice Statistics, Juristat: Homicide in Canada, for the years 2001-04. The gun ownership data come from Graduate Institute of International Studies (2003). Small Arms Survey, 2003. Oxford University Press, pp. 64 and 65, tables 2.2 ("Known Civilian Firearms in the European Union") and 2.3 ("Known Civilian Firearms in Other European Countries").

2. A few statistics in this table were corrected for errors, specifically, the murder rate for Luxembourg and the gun ownership rate for Germany.

Canadian demography does not support the claim that the more guns a community has the more murders it has (table 4). The Atlantic provinces have a relatively high number of gun owners per capita, but among the lowest homicide rates in the country. At the other extreme, BC has fewer households with firearms than the national average, but a relatively high homicide rate.

American demographic data also refute the myth that fewer guns in a community mean less murder. The murder rate among African-Americans is six times higher than among whites. Does this mean African-Americans have more guns? No. Ordinary law-abiding African-Americans are markedly less likely than whites to own guns. But the argument for banning guns to everyone is refuted, since fewer guns for law-abiding African-Americans does not mean fewer guns for African-American criminals. Incidentally, rural African-Americans own guns as frequently as whites, but the murder rate among them is only a tiny fraction of the urban African-American rate (Kates and Mauser, 2007, pp. 676-677).[4]

Table 2: Murder Rates of European Nations that Ban Handguns, as Compared to their Neighbors that Allow Handguns (per 100,000 persons)

NATION	HANDGUN POLICY	MURDER RATE	YEAR
A. Belarus	banned	10.4	late 1990s
Neighbors for which gun law and murder rate data are available			
Poland	allowed	1.98	2003
Russia	banned	20.54	2002
B. Luxembourg	banned	9.01	2002
Neighbors for which gun law and murder rate data are available			
Belgium	allowed	1.7	late 1990s
France	allowed	1.65	2003
Germany	allowed	0.93	2003
C. Russia	banned	20.54	2002
Neighbors for which gun law and murder rate data are available			
Finland	allowed	1.98	2004
Norway	allowed	0.81	2001

Sources: Dauvergne, 2003, 2004; Graduate Institute of International Studies, 2003; Savoie, 2002; United Nations Office on Drugs and Crime, 2004.

Table 3: North American Gun Ownership Rates and Homicide Rates in 2001

	Gun ownership rate	Homicide rate
Canada	36,349	1.78
US	89,116	5.62
Mexico	9,709	13.94

Source: Gun ownership rate: Graduate Institute of International Studies (2003). "Table 2.4: The Deadliest Gun Use. Stockpile Lethality in Nine Latin American Countries, with Selected Examples from Elsewhere." In Chapter 2, *Small Arms Survey*, 2003. Oxford University Press. Homicide rates data come from police data. For Canada: Canadian Centre for Justice Statistics (2001) *Homicide in Canada*. For the US: Federal Bureau of Investigation (2001), *Index of Crime in the US*. For Mexico covering the period 2000-2001: United Nations, Office of Drugs and Crime, Division for Policy Analysis and Public Affairs. *The Eighth United Nations Survey of Crime Trends and Operations of Criminal Justice Systems*

Table 4: Homicide Rate and Household Gun Ownership for Canadian Provinces[1]

	Homicide rate	Percent of households owning firearms[1]
Atlantic[2]	1.62	28
Quebec	1.32	18
Ontario	1.74	13
Manitoba	4.16	21
Saskatchewan	4.33	25
Alberta	3.35	17
British Columbia	2.30	15
Territories[2]	2.89	41
CANADA	**2.04**	**17**

1. Column 3 updated on January 15, 2008 to correct error.
2. The Atlantic provinces and the territories have been grouped into regional categories because the GPC 2000 survey of firearms ownership did not distinguish between provinces or territories in these regions.
Sources: Populations and homicide data from *Juristat* (2005), *Crime in Canada*. Firearm ownership from GPC Research, 2001.

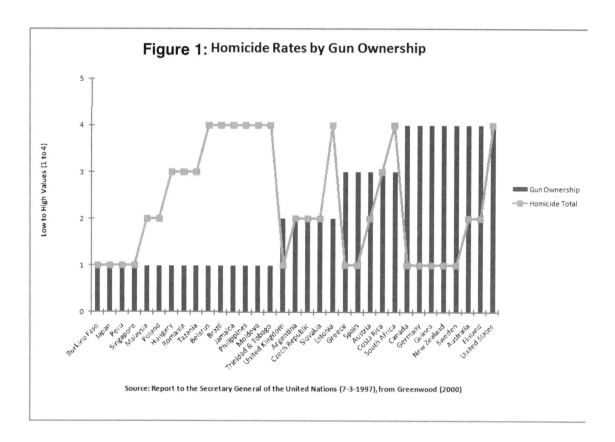

Figure 1: Homicide Rates by Gun Ownership

Source: Report to the Secretary General of the United Nations (7-3-1997), from Greenwood (2000)

Regardless of race, the distinction between good people and criminals is vital. It is utterly false that most murderers are ordinary people who went wrong because they had guns. The overwhelming majority of murderers have life histories of violence, restraining orders, substance abuse problems, form of psychopathology.5 It is generally illegal for such people to have guns, but unlike good people, they ignore gun laws—just as they ignore laws against violence.

The "more guns mean more murders" mythology also flies in the face of history. A few nineteenth century American states adopted gun controls because they had (and still have) severe violent crime rates. In most states, murders were few despite high gun ownership and virtually no gun control. Likewise, Europe had low murder rates prior to World War I despite high gun ownership and virtually no controls. Severe European gun laws appeared (for political reasons) in the tumultuous post-World War I era. Despite ever-stricter gun laws, both political and apolitical violence has increased apace in Europe (Kates and Mauser, 2007, pp. 678-685; Malcolm, 2002).

If anything, a review of the European experience demonstrates more guns correlating with less murder. Nine European nations (including Germany, Austria, Denmark, and Norway) have more than 15,000 guns per 100,000 members of the population. Nine others (including Luxembourg, Russia, and Hungary) have fewer than 5,000 guns per 100,000 members of the population. But the aggregate murder rates of these nine low-gun-ownership nations are three times higher than those of the nine high-gun-ownership nations.

Some might argue that this shows how widespread gun ownership actually reduces violence rates.

There is substantial evidence that this is true in the United States, where gun ownership for self-defense is very common (Lott and Mustard, 1997; Kleck, 1997, pp. 184-186). In addition, there is some evidence that a small number of Canadians do likewise (Mauser, 1996). But there is no evidence that Norwegians, Germans, and other Europeans often keep guns for defense.

The reason that nations (or regions within nations) with more guns tend to have lower violence is political rather than criminological. Gun ownership generally has no effect on how much violent crime a society has. Violent crime is determined by fundamental economic and socio-cultural factors, not the mere availability of just one of a bevy of potential murder instruments. Politicians in nations with severe crime problems often think that banning guns will be a quick fix. But gun bans don't work; if anything, they make things worse. They disarm the law-abiding, yet are ignored by the violent and the criminal. Yet nations with severe violence problems tend to have severe gun laws. For example, both Jamaica and the Republic of Ireland banned all firearms in the 1970s, but homicide and gun homicide have continued to increase (Mauser, 2007). By the same token, the murder rates in handgun-banning US cities including New York, Chicago, and Washington, DC are far higher than in states like Pennsylvania and Connecticut, where handguns are legal and widely owned.

In sum, banning guns for the general public increases people's vulnerability and fails to reduce violence because the law-abiding citizenry are victims of violent crime, not perpetrators. Banning guns for violent criminals, juveniles, and the insane (which both Canadian and American laws already do) is good policy, though such laws are very difficult to enforce. As I argued in 2006, the government should immediately create a list of high-risk individuals (for example, convicted violent criminals, including parolees, and persons with an outstanding criminal arrest warrant) and encourage both the RCMP and Immigration Canada to use it to monitor dangerous offenders (Mauser, 2006). Disarming those who only want to defend themselves, however, merely empowers criminals at the expense of the innocent.

NOTES

* This article originally appeared in the Fraser Forum, October 2007, pp 23-27, published by the Fraser Institute, Vancouver, BC, Canada. Reprinted with permission of the author.

1. Some earlier studies that examined the relationship between national levels of gun ownership and homicide rates across a number of countries are Greenwood, 2000; Killias et al., 2001; Kleck, 1997; and Miron, 2001. Despite the differences in methodology and the ideological biases of the authors, none of these studies reported finding a significant relationship between national levels of gun ownership and homicide rates.

2. Homicides in England and Wales (the largest region in Great Britain) averaged 703 per year during the five years prior to the handgun ban (with 54 involving firearms), but increased to 895 per year (with 61 involving firearms) for the five-year period ending in 2005 (Walker et al., 2006, table 2.04, p. 30). The other major jurisdiction in Great Britain is Scotland, where the homicide rate increased even more during this same time period.

3. This figure is based upon Colin Greenwood's (2000) analysis of data supplied to the United Nations. The quality of these data are "as supplied" by the country and consequently, vary considerably. Homicide has a few distinct definitions and the numbers of gun owners have been estimated using various methodologies. In his analysis, Greenwood categorized the data sets into four levels of magnitude, from low to high.

4. Kates and Mauser drew upon several studies that examined crime rates by race in the United States, e.g., Blumstein, 1995, pp. 10, 21; Kleck, 1997, p. 71; and Fingerhut et al., 1992, pp. 3048 and 3049, table 1.

5. Numerous studies have replicated this finding. A few of these are: Myers and Scott, 1998, pp. 160-63; Langford, Isaac, and Adams, 2000, in Blackman, pp. 51, 55, 59; Straus, 1986, pp. 446, 454, 457. In Canada, almost two-thirds of adults accused of homicide are known to have a Canadian criminal record (see Dauvergne and Li, 2006, p. 11).

REFERENCES

Blumstein, Alfred (1995). "Youth Violence, Guns and the Illicit-Drug Industry." *Journal of Criminal Law and Criminology* 86: 10-36.

Dauvergne, Mia (2003). "Homicide in Canada." *Juristat 24*, 8: 3.

Dauvergne, Mia (2004). "Homicide in Canada." *Juristat 25*, 6: 3.

Dauvergne, Mia and Geoffrey Li (2006). "Homicide in Canada, 2005." *Juristat 26*, 6. Statistics Canada.

Fingerhut, Lois A. et al. (1992). "Firearm and Non Firearm Homicide among Persons 15 through 19 Years of Age." *Journal of the American Medical Association* 267: 3048.

GPC Research (2001). Fall 2000 Estimate of Firearms Ownership. Ottawa: Canadian Firearms Centre (January 2). Graduate Institute of International Studies (2003). Small Arms Survey 2003. Geneva. Greenwood, Colin. Cross Sectional Study of the Relationship Between Levels of Gun Ownership and Violent Deaths (March). West Yorkshire, England: Firearms Research and Advisory Service. Kari, Shannon (2007). "Liberals Add 200 OPP Officers to Fight Gun Crime." National Post (July 27). Digital document available at *http://www.canada.com/ nationalpost/news/story.html?id=8ad91198 -0b4c-4d73-a1c4-38306ad129cd&k=14547.*

Kates, Don and Gary Mauser (2007). "Would Banning Firearms Reduce Murder and Suicide? A Review of International Evidence." *Harvard Journal of Law and Public Policy*, 30: 651-694.

Killias, Martin et al. (2001). "Guns, Violent Crime, and Suicide in 21 Countries," *Canadian Journal of Criminology and Criminal Justice* 43: 429, 430.

Kleck, Gary (1997). *Targeting Guns: Firearms and their Control.* New York: de Greyter.

Langford, Linda, Isaac Adams, Nancy Adams, and Sandra Adams (2000). "Criminal and Restraining Order Histories of Intimate Partner-Related Homicide Offenders in Massachusetts, 1991-95." In Paul Blackman, V.L. Leggett, B.I. Olson, and J.P. Jarvis, eds. *The Varieties of Homicide and its Research: Proceedings of the 1999 Meeting of the Homicide Research Working Group.* Washington, DC: Federal Bureau of Investigation.

Lott, John R. and David B. Mustard (1997). "Crime, Deterrence and Right to Carry." *Journal of Legal Studies* 26: 1-68.

Malcolm, Joyce (2002). *Guns and Violence: The English Experience.* Harvard University Press.

Mauser, Gary (1996). "Armed Self Defense: The Canadian Case." *Journal of Criminal Justice 24*, 5: 393-406.

Mauser, Gary (2006). "After the Gun Registry." Fraser Forum (May): 18-20.

Mauser, Gary. "Do Restrictive Firearm Laws Improve Public Safety?" *Economic Affairs, Special Edition on Prohibitions.* London, England: Institute of Economic Affairs.

Miron, Jeffrey A. (2001). "Violence, Guns, and Drugs: A Cross-Country Analysis." *Journal of Law and Economics* 44: 615, 625ff.

Myers, Wade C. and Kerrilyn Scott (1998). "Psychotic and Conduct Disorder Symptoms in Juvenile Murderers." *Homicide Studies 2,* 160: 161-63.

Savoie, Josee (2002). "Homicide in Canada." *Juristat 23,* 8: 3.

Straus, Murray A. (1986). "Domestic Violence and Homicide Antecedents." *Bulletin of the NY Academy of Medicine* 62.

UK News (2007). "Rhys Murder Shows Crime is 'Out of Control'." August 23. Digital document available at *http://www.lifestyleextra.com/ShowStory.as p?story=XT234120000&news_headline= rhys_murder_shows_crime_is_out_of_ control.*

United Nations (1997). *Report to the Secretary General of the United Nations by the Economic and Social Council, Commission on Crime Prevention and Criminal Justice.* E/CN 15/1997/4, 7 (March).

United Nations Office on Drugs and Crime (2004). *The Seventh United Nations Survey on Crime Trends and the Operations of Criminal Justice Systems (1998–2000)* (March 31). New York: 82, 260, 287, 370, 405, 398.

Walker, Allison, Chris Kershaw, and Sian Nicholas (2006). *Crime in England and Wales, 2005/06.* Home Office Statistical Bulletin no 12/06 (July). London, England: Home Office.

CROSS SECTIONAL STUDY OF THE RELATIONSHIP BETWEEN LEVELS OF GUN OWNERSHIP AND VIOLENT DEATHS

COLIN GREENWOOD

The proposition that, "places with the highest rates of gun ownership and the most virulent opposition to gun control are the very places with the highest rates of gun deaths" [1] has been tested against the latest available research which covers no less than thirty three different countries and is based on information supplied to the United Nations by the countries concerned and assembled by a team of researchers supplied by the Government of Canada[2].

The figures supplied have been placed into bands representing (a) very low levels, (b) low levels, (c) high levels and (d) very high levels under each category for gun ownership, homicide, gun homicide, suicide, gun suicide and accidents. The following table summarises the results. Whilst the figures used are 'as reported' and have not been corrected for many possible variables, the results are placed into broad bands with very wide differentials.

The table shows that the United States has a very high level of gun ownership and also has high or very high levels of homicide, gun homicide, gun suicide and gun accidents. But that one example does not establish an immutable rule. Australia, Canada, Finland, Germany, New Zealand and Sweden all have very high levels of gun ownership, inland's being the highest recorded in the survey. All these are matched with low or very low levels of homicide, with very low accident levels in all but one case, and with very variable suicide rates.

This survey confirms that, despite a single exception, a high level of violent deaths and particularly guns deaths can exist in countries where gun ownership levels vary from very low to very high and that very low levels of violent deaths can exist in countries with very high levels of gun ownership.

There is, in fact, no relationship between high levels of gun ownership and high levels of gun deaths or of violent deaths in general.

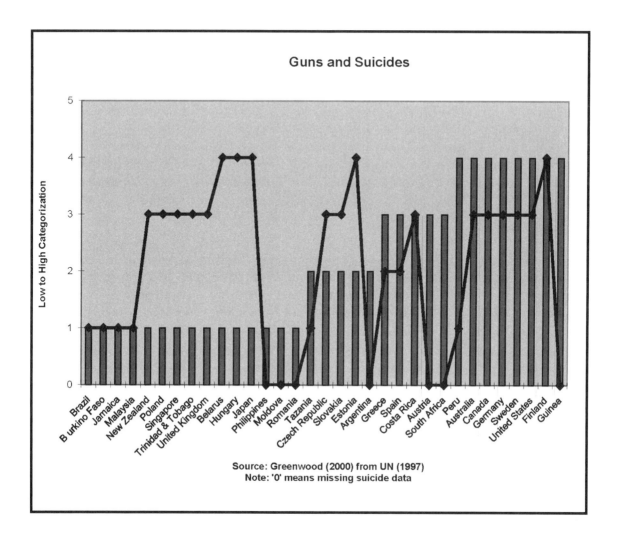

Guns and Suicides

Source: Greenwood (2000) from UN (1997)
Note: '0' means missing suicide data

TABLE: GUN HOMICIDE SUICIDE GUN

Country	Gun Ownership	Homicide Total	Gun	Suicide Total	Gun	Gun Accidents
Argentina	b	b	b	*	*	*
Australia	d	b	a	c	c	a
Austria	c	b	a	*	*	*
Belarus	a	d	-	d	*	b
Brazil	a	d	d	a	a	
Burkino Faso	a	a	*		a	a
Canada	d	a	a	c	c	a
Costa Rica	c	c	b	c	b	b
Czech Republic	b	b	a	c	b	a
Estonia	b	d	c	d	c	d
Finland	d	b	a	d	d	a
Germany	d	a	a	c	b	a
Greece	c	a	a	b	b	a
Guinea	d	a	*	*	*	*
Hungary	a	c	a	d	a	*
Jamaica	a	d	d	a	a	a
Japan	a	a		d	a	a
Malaysia	a	b	a	a	a	a
New Zealand	d	a	a	c	c	b
Peru	a	a	b	a	a	a
Philippines	a	d	c	*	*	*
Poland	a	b	a	c	a	a
Moldova	a	d	a	*	*	*
Romania	a	c	a	*	*	*
Singapore	a	a	a	c	*	*
Slovakia	b	b	a	c	a	*
South Africa	c	d	d	*	*	*
Spain	c	a	a	b	a	b
Sweden	d	a	a	c	b	a
Tanzania	a	c	a	a	a	a
Trinidad & Tobago	a	d	c	c	a	d
United Kingdom	b	a	a	c	a	a
United States	d	d	c	c	d	d

(a) - Very Low. (b) - Low (c) - High (d) - Very High * No figure.

Table extracted from the Report to the Secretary General of the United Nations by the Economic and Social Council, Commission on Crime Prevention and Criminal Justice in 1997, 7th March 1997, E/CN.15/1997/4.

INTRODUCTION

The proposition that, "places with the highest rates of gun ownership and the most virulent opposition to gun control are the very places with the highest rates of gun deaths" [1] is frequently advanced as if it were some immutable law of nature, akin to a asserting that the sun always rises in the east and sets in the west. The latter claim can be verified by complex scientific study of the relationship between the earth and the sun, but it can be verified more easily by observation in every country in the world, and in every part of each country, where it will be found to be the case. Such verification would be called a cross sectional study. The proposition about the sun can also be verified by a time series study, that is to say that in one place, the sun has been observed to follow this law for all time.

But the claim of a relationship between gun ownership levels and gun deaths is rarely supported by evidence. It is claimed as natural law without logic or rational verification. The quoted claim appears to have been made in the course of high profile journalistic cover of a particular event, but it is advanced as a means of social engineering by those who wish to control the actions and the thinking of populations. It is also used as a crutch for those responsible for the control of crime who, by accepting the validity of the claim, seek to gain political advantage by imposing simple 'remedies'.

If the proposition is valid it must hold good across many countries, and across time in any single country. It must also work in reverse and places or times with the fewest firearms must have the lowest level of gun deaths.

A time series study, testing the proposition over time in a single area, may be the simplest test, but even that will have to be corrected for variables such as major changes in the nature of the society, changes in law, social attitudes, police efficiency in combating crime, judicial systems and crime recording methods.

The proposition should also be able to withstand a valid and thorough cross sectional analysis, but this is much more complex. Any study would have to correct for variations in gun counting systems, crime counting systems, demographics, history, relative police efficiency, variables in the judicial systems, social attitudes and much more. If those variables can be fully taken into account, the proposition must remain valid across many countries and not merely in respect of samples carefully selected by researchers to validate a predetermined theory.

A study which encompasses a long period or a large number of countries would be valid if the proposition was supported in the vast majority of instances and rational explanation was available for a very small number of exceptions.

The purpose of any study must be, firstly, to establish levels of gun ownership over time in a particular country, or at any one time in a truly representative series of countries. Secondly, to establish levels of gun deaths, usually sub divided into homicide, suicide and accidents. Finally, it must be demonstrated that the two things are causally related.

GUN OWNERSHIP LEVELS

Many different methods have been used to establish gun ownership levels. Perhaps the most bizarre was based on a telephone survey and later used in a much quoted analysis of the relationship between gun ownership and homicide in selected countries.[3] It seems highly unlikely to say the least that gun owners would respond with any degree of accuracy to a telephone call from a researcher on a subject which is generally seen as highly sensitive.

Gun ownership levels have also been estimated from licences issued by the authorities, but the nature of gun controls vary widely and guns which are licensed in one country are completely free from control in another. In Britain, all classes of shotguns are licensed and must be accounted for individually. In France, most shotguns are free from any control. One survey comparing a Canadian City with a nearby city in the United States City was flawed by an assumption that, at the time, the number of Canadian licences gave an indication of the number of guns when, in fact, it provided only an authority to acquire an additional gun or guns and took no account of existing stocks.[4]

But even in countries where a strict licensing regime has been in force over a long period the number of guns within that system is almost certain to be a gross understatement of the number of guns available in that society. At one level, licences take no account of guns in the hands of military, police and others. State servants, like all other people, are involved in crimes and suicides and in some countries appear to have a marked propensity for accidents. In many countries, militia firearms are widely available to citizens.

The extent to which even the strictest firearms registration system accurately reflects the number of guns in private hands is a matter for grave doubt. A licensing system in Victoria, Australia had licensed only the person but in 1984 new legislation required the registration of all guns. A 1987 report by the firearms registrar indicated that after three years only 58.9% of firearms he conservatively estimated to have been in licensed hands had been registered. The remaining firearms were still in circulation, probably in non criminal hands, but outside the new system of control.[5] The report remained unknown except to police and politicians until it was discovered by means of freedom of information laws It was later sidelined by further legislation in the wake of the 1996 Port Arthur shootings.

In Britain prior to 1988, magazine shotguns were treated in the same way as all other shotguns and subject only to the licensing of the individual with no registration of the guns. New legislation required registration of all shotguns and made some classes of magazine shotguns subject to much stricter controls. Estimates from the British trade obtained by The Shooting Sports Trust, indicated that at least 300,000 such guns had been sold in the preceding ten years alone, with many more sold prior to that. Not more than 50,000 of the guns were registered under the new laws and a further small number may have been otherwise disposed of. The evidence indicates that about a quarter of a million such guns remain illegally in circulation.[6]

There is nothing to suggest that these observations on compliance rates for gun registration are other than entirely representative. Estimates for the number of unregistered guns in Britain have been based on factors such as the number of unregistered guns confiscated by or surrendered to the police, and the evidence suggests that the number of illegally held guns is at least as great as the number legally held.[7] But the total number of guns registered or unregistered in society is not related to the numbers of such guns possessed or used by criminals, including killers. In most countries those with certain criminal convictions will be prohibited from owning guns, yet the evidence is that it is just this class of person which accounts for the greater part of crime, including fatal crime.[8] Evidence about the sources of this relatively small number of firearms in any country is incomplete and studies have, in particular, failed to explore the extent to which legal action against one source will simply result in a shift of source.

Where gun licensing is the exception rather than the rule, estimates of gun ownership levels may be based on the number of guns manufactured and imported, but can take no account of guns illegally imported, or indeed, illegally manufactured. They are not usually corrected for wastage and fail to account for guns in the hands of the servants of the State.

GUNS DEATHS

It seems to be assumed that producing comparable time series or cross sectional figures for gun deaths is a simple matter. In fact truly comparable statistics are almost impossible to produce. It is further assumed that reducing deaths by guns would also reduce total deaths. The evidence does not support that assumption and a reduction in gun deaths would only be beneficial if it produced a reduction in overall deaths and was not simply the cause of a switch to other methods of killing.

Until recently those seeking to highlight a problem with gun ownership levels concentrated attention on the claimed relationship with gun homicide levels and sometimes with general homicide levels in various countries. More recently, there have been claims that both gun suicide and general suicide levels are related to levels of gun ownership and that gun accident levels are subject to the same causes.

HOMICIDE

The Home Office is responsible for collecting statistics relating to England and Wales whilst Scotland and Northern Ireland statistics are separately collected and presented. Since 1967, The Home Office has 'adjusted' homicide statistics retrospectively by taking account of the decisions of the courts or the prosecuting authorities. The number of recorded homicides is reduced by between 13% and 15% by this process. Few other countries reduce the statistics in this way and in many, deaths which are clearly self defence or for which some other defence exists are recorded as homicide. In England and Wales causing death by dangerous driving is no longer regarded as homicide reducing the figure by some 200 cases per year. In many countries that offence falls into the homicide classification. Recording practices also vary in respect of attempted homicide; criminal statistics for Russia, France and Switzerland used in some studies included attempts as reported homicides, whilst in Portugal cases in which the cause of death is unknown have been shown as homicide, inflating their figure considerably.[9]

Steps have been taken through the Council of Europe to make homicide statistics in Western Europe broadly comparable but many existing studies are based on older figures where the differences in recording practice will distort any comparison. England is generally cited as having an extremely low homicide rate, but in existing studies, the figure would have to be increased by about 30% for comparison with figures for some other countries and should be almost doubled for comparison with those countries which have included attempts with homicide for the purposes of earlier studies.

SUICIDE

Suicide levels appear to be reported more consistently than gun ownership or homicide levels, though there remains a difficulty in a proportion of cases in which the reason for the death is less than clear. Some cases which are suicide may be reported as accidental deaths for a variety of reasons and there is likely to be an absence of consistency. Reporting in many third world countries may be much less than complete and less accurate than it is amongst Western Countries.

Many variables influence suicide rates including religion, social norms and history. Many methods of committing suicide are readily to hand and two different questions therefore arise. The first is whether there is a causal relationship between the number of guns in a society and the rate of suicide in general or gun suicide in particular; the second is whether a reduction in gun numbers, if that could be achieved, is likely to secure a reduction in overall suicide or whether it would merely lead to the substitution of another method with no saving of life.

The great mass of evidence indicates that the suicide rate is not dependent on the availability of one method and that if, by some means, all firearms could be removed from a society, the rate of suicide would remain largely unchanged. The only evidence to the contrary was generated by the change from toxic domestic gas (which had been a significant method of suicide) to non toxic natural gas. Studies in several countries suggested that, though this had resulted in a significant reduction in gas suicides, there had been no overall reduction in suicide rates. One exception was a study in England by Clarke and Mayhew [10] which found that the change had caused a significant reduction in overall suicide, though a later study by the same authors suggested that the same was not true for Scotland.

The latest analysis of available evidence, which includes a critique of the Clarke and Mayhew study is that done by Professor Gary Kleck [11] who found that Clarke and Mayhew's conclusions could not be supported by the evidence. The now dated time series analyses of suicide figures for England and Wales over a long period [12] shows that the suicide rate has been unaffected by massive reductions in gun ownership levels.

ACCIDENTAL GUN DEATHS

If there were no guns, there could be no accidental gun deaths, but it does not necessarily follow that the number of gun deaths is causally related to the volume of gun ownership. As with other causes of death, analysis of accidents is more complex that it first appears. Accidental deaths include a number involving military or police personnel and state owned guns. Most countries have very low levels of gun accidents, and factors other than the mere availability of guns may be significant. However this is the cause of death which, in theory, is most likely to be associated with levels of gun ownership.

UN SURVEY

The most extensive survey of legal firearms ownership was carried out by researchers provided by the Government of Canada under the auspices of the United Nations Economic and Social Council, Commission on Crime Prevention and Criminal Justice in 1997 and is published as a report to the Secretary General on 25th April 1997 as E/CN.15/1997/4. It surveyed the largest number of countries yet attempted to obtain comparative figures for gun ownership levels and gun related deaths. A number of countries supplied details only of gun ownership levels and, since they cannot form part of any comparison, they have been excluded. Thirty three countries provided some measure of gun ownership and a measure of least one class of gun deaths.

The numbers reported in every category span a very wide range and a small number of countries reporting very high numbers in any category tended to bias the more usual attempts to fit the numbers into comparative bands. Bands which distinguished between countries with low and moderate sets of numbers are therefore employed in this analysis, but the reported numbers are also included so that the bands can be re-calculated if that is thought appropriate.

GUN OWNERSHIP

Details of firearms ownership are reported in terms of the numbers per 100,000 of (1) firearms licences, (2) firearms owners and (3) firearms. It also sought to establish (4) the proportion of households in which at least one person owned a gun. Responses varied over the range of 0.1 to 411 legally held firearms per 100,000 people and from 0.2% to 50% of households with one gun owner.

Because of the variables already outlined and because of the shortcomings of the survey itself, it would be appropriate to consider the results in terms of bands of numbers of firearms per 100,000 (a) very low - 0 to 24.99, (b) low - 25 to 49.99 (c) high - 50 to 99.99 and (d) very high - 100 to the reported maximum of 411. Where the number of firearms was not given, countries have been placed into bands on the basis of one of the other headings with an indication of which of the headings (1) to (4) above is used.

Band (a) 0 to 24.99 firearms per 100,000 population - very low

Belarus 16.5: Brazil 8.18 (2): Burkino Faso 0.24: Hungary 15.54: Jamaica 7.35: Japan 3.28: Malaysia 7.05: Peru 7.65: Philippines 6.97: Poland 5.30: Moldova 6.61: Romania 2.97: Singapore 0.24: Trinidad and Tobago 6.06: Tanzania 2.33.

Band (b) 25 to 49.99 firearms per 100,000 population - low
Argentina 41.59: Czech Republic 27.58: Estonia 28.56: Slovakia 31.91: United Kingdom 36.58.

Band (c) 50 to 99.99 firearms per 1000,000 population - high
Austria 41.02(1)*: Costa Rica 65.95: Greece 77.00: Spain 64.69: South Africa 84.41.
*An Austrian licence may cover several firearms.

Band (d) 100 to 411 firearms per 100,000 population - very high
Australia 195.90: Canada 241.48: Finland 411.20: Germany 122.56(2):
Guinea 108.86(2): New Zealand 308.90: Sweden 246.65: United States 41% (4)#

#The figure of 41% of households in the United States is marginally less than the 50% in Finland, but greater than the remaining countries in this band. The number of firearms per 100,000 must therefore fall into this highest band. Elsewhere some scholars report actual gun ownership levels which may be as high as 900 per 1,000 people.[13]

Unfortunately, figures for a number of important countries, particularly European countries such as Switzerland, France and Holland do not yet appear in UN statistics. It is possible to reflect, however, that very low levels of legal gun ownership appear in many countries which are less developed or currently less stable, though there are clear exceptions to that statement. High levels of legal gun ownership appear more common in developed and stable democracies.

The figures presented here are provided by the governments concerned. The variables in reporting practices and other factors are corrected for to some extent by the use of wide bands of the figures and by the fact that they are compared only with figures for deaths derived from the same sources.

GUN DEATHS

The UN study attempts a broad based cross sectional study of gun deaths which is fraught with complexities. The quality of recording methods in many third world countries is questionable, but even amongst the most advanced countries major differences in recording methods make comparisons of gun death rates extremely difficult. If these figures are also employed in broad bands they may provide a cross sectional analysis at least as valid as any other that has been attempted.

HOMICIDE

International comparisons based on homicide rates are highly susceptible to distortion and the UN Survey cautions that homicide figures are 'as reported' and subject to the strictures set out above. As with figures for levels of gun ownership or numbers of guns the range of figures reported is enormous and they are considered in broad bands. To avoid distortion by a small number of very high figures, the bands show the total number of homicides per hundred thousand population in four bands - (a) 0 to 0.99 - very low; (b) 2 to 3.99 - low; (c) 4 to 7.99 - high and (d) 8+ - very high. Actual figures are included to allow of redistribution within the bands.

Homicides per 100,000 population in band (a) - very low
Burkina Faso 0.04: Canada 1.99: Germany 1.81: Greece 1.33: Guinea 0.34:
Japan 0.60: New Zealand 1.35: Peru 1.41: Singapore 1.62: Spain 1.58: Sweden 1.35:
United Kingdom 1.40.

Homicides per 100,000 population in band (b) - low
Argentina 3.83: Australia 2.40: Austria 2.14: Czech Republic 2.80: Finland 3.25:
Malaysia 2.13: Poland 2.61: Slovakia 2.38.

Homicides per 100,000 population in band (c) - high
Costa Rica 5.52: Hungary 4.07: Romania 4.32: Tanzania 7.42.

Homicides per 100,000 population in band (d) - very high
Belarus 9.86: Brazil 29.17: Estonia 22.11: Jamaica 31.60: Philippines 16.89:
Moldova 17.06: South Africa 64.64: Trinidad and Tobago 9.48: United States 8.95.

Gun homicide figures are reported separately and these are also shown in four bands; (a) 0. to 0.99 - very low; (b) 1 to 2.99 - low; (c) 3 to 6.99 - high and (d) 7 + - very high.

Gun homicides per 100,000 population in band (a) - very low
Australia 0.56: Austria 0.53: Canada 0.60: Czech Republic 0.92: Finland 0.87:
Germany 0.21: Greece 0.55: Guinea 0.03: Hungary 0.47: Japan 0.03:
Malaysia 0.20: New Zealand 0.22: Poland 0.27: Moldova 0.63: Romania 0.12:
Singapore 0.00: Slovakia 0.36: Spain 0.19: Sweden 0.31: United Kingdom 0.13:
Tanzania 0.50.

Gun homicides per 100,000 population in band (b) - low
Argentina 1.50: Costa Rica 2.57: Peru 1.06.

Gun homicides per 100,000 population in band (c) - high
Estonia 6.12: Philippines 3.61: Trinidad and Tobago 3.42: United States 6.24.

Gun homicides per 100,000 population in band (d) - very high
Brazil 25.78: Jamaica 18.23: South Africa 26.63.

SUICIDE

The UN Survey reports the following overall suicide rates per 100,000 populations which are placed in the four bands shown for the reasons set out above: (a) 0 to 1.99 very low, (b) 2 to 5.99 - low, (c) 6 to 15.99 - high, and (d) 16+ - very high.

Suicides per 100,000 population in band (a) - 0 to 1.99 - very low
Brazil 0.63: Burkino Faso 0.95: Jamaica 1.46: Malaysia 1.83: Peru 0.42: Tanzania 0.88.

Suicides per 100,000 population in band (b) - 2 to 5.99 - low
Greece 3.54: Spain 5.92.

Suicides per 100,000 population in band (c) - 6 to 15.99 - high
Australia 12.77: Canada 12.88: Costa Rica 6.54: Czech Republic 9.88:
Germany 15.80: New Zealand 13.81: Poland 14.23: Singapore 9.89: Slovakia 13.24:
Sweden 15.65: Trinidad and Tobago 8.08: United Kingdom 7.55:
United States 11.54.

Suicides per 100,000 population in band (d) - 16+ - very high
Belarus 27.26: Estonia 39.99: Finland 27.28: Hungary 33.34: Japan 17.95.

Suicides involving firearms per 100,000 populations are also shown in four bands (a) 0 to 0.99 - very low, (b) 1 to 1.99 - low, (c) 2 to 3.99 - high, and (d) 4+ - very high.

Gun suicides per 100,000 population in band (a) - 0 to 0.99 - very low
Brazil 0.44: Burkino Faso 0.14: Hungary 0.88: Jamaica 0.36: Japan 0.04:
Malaysia 0.00: Peru 0.10: Poland 0.16: Slovakia 0.58 Spain 0.55:
Trinidad and Tobago 0.08: United Kingdom 0.33: Tanzania 0.02.

Gun Suicides per 100,000 population in band (b) - 1 to 1.99 - low
Costa Rica 1.61: Czech Republic 1.01: Germany 1.23: Greece 1.30: Sweden 1.95.

Gun suicides per 100,000 population in band (c) - 2 to 3.99 - high
Australia 2.38: Canada 3.35: Estonia 3.63. New Zealand 2.45.

Gun suicides per 100,000 population in band (d) - 4+ - very high
Finland 5.78: United States 7.23.

The UN analysis contains details of overall suicide rates and firearm suicide rates, and if the weapon-substitution theory set out above is even partially correct, then any conclusions should be drawn on the basis of overall suicide rates and not on the basis of gun suicide rates only, but both suicide rates are included in this study.

GUN ACCIDENTS

Fatal firearms accidents are shown for many countries, but these are all extremely low. For reasons set out above, four bands of the number of accidents per 100,000 population have again been created: (a) 0 to 0.19 - very low (b) 0.2 to 0.29 - low (c) 0.3 to 0.39 high and over 0.4 - very high.

Gun accidents per 100,000 population in band (a) - 0 to 0.19 - very low
Australia 0.11: Burkino Faso 0.05: Canada 0.13: Czech Republic 0.07: Finland 0.12: Germany 0.03: Greece 0.02: Jamaica 0.12: Japan 0.02: Malaysia 0.08: Peru 0.02: Poland 0.01: Sweden 0.05: United Kingdom 0.02: Tanzania 0.02.

Gun accidents per 100,000 population in band (b) - 0.2 to 0.29 - low
Belarus 0.23: Costa Rica 0.29: Spain 0.26. New Zealand 0.29.

Gun accidents per 100,000 population in band (c) - 0.3 to 0.39 - high
None

Gun accidents per 100,000 population in band (d) - 0.4+ - very high
Brazil 0.75: Estonia 0.40: Trinidad and Tobago 0.54: United States 0.58.

COMPARISON

To test the assertion that countries with high levels of gun ownership either invariably or usually have high levels of gun deaths, the information has been tabulated according to the bands described above.

COMMENTARY

Examination of the table based on the UN survey shows that the United States has a very high level of gun ownership and also has very high levels of homicide, gun suicide and gun accidents but with high level of gun homicide. But that one example does not establish an invariable rule. Australia, Canada, Finland, Germany, New Zealand and Sweden all have very high levels of gun ownership, Finland's being the highest recorded in the survey. All these are matched with low or very low levels of homicide, with very low accident levels in all but one case and with very variable suicide rates.

FOOTNOTES

Comment not forming part of the UN Survey may further amplify the results.

(1) The unique status of the United States is further highlighted by the enormous variations in homicide rates within that country. Detailed cross sectional analysis within the United States would be illuminating, but space allows only of perhaps extreme examples. Lott14 identifies the ten States with the lowest rates of homicide per 100,000 in 1992 as Alaska, 3.2, Utah 2.99, Massachusetts 2.97, Montana 2.22, North Dakota 1.9, Maine 1.7, New Hampshire 1.5, Iowa 1.1, Vermont 0.7 and South Dakota 0.6. In the bands used in this paper, six of those States would have very low levels and four low levels of homicide. Conversely, the ten States with the highest levels of homicide clearly fell into the very high band.

(2) The rate of accidental gun deaths in the United States is shown in the UN Survey as
0.58 per 100,000 and falls into the very high band. Other statistics indicate that this apparent relationship between a pair of figures in a single country does not justify the claim of a causal relationship. United States Government figures for fatal gun accidents are available from 1933 and show that the rate has been consistently declining from 2.40 deaths per 100,000 population in 1933 to 0.47 in 1995, the figures for 1945 being 1.84 and that for 1994 being 0.4715. During the period 1945 to 1994, the total stock of guns in the United States has risen from about 49 million to 235 million.13 If the relationship is causal, it would be possible to conclude that more guns generate fewer fatal gun accidents, but no such suggestion would be made here.

(3) The United Kingdom introduced strict controls on some firearms in 1920 and has pursued a programme of continuously increasing those controls, significantly reducing its level of legitimate firearms ownership. In the ten years from 1988 to 1997, the number of licenced gun owners in England and Wales has been reduced by 27% from 1,037,400 to 756,700.16 In 1919, when firearms were effectively free from control in England and Wales, the homicide rate was 0.8 per 100,000 whilst that for the United States was 9.5 (11.9 times higher).**17** The UN Survey shows a rate of 1.40 for Great Britain, but the figure for England and Wales for 1995 is 1.35 per 100,00018 whilst in the Survey the USA is shown to have a figure of 8.95 (6.62 times higher). For an accurate comparison the number for England and Wales should probably be substantially greater than that shown. The comparative advantage which England had against the USA in homicide figures has actually been significantly reduced.

(4) Japan reported a very high overall suicide rate for this survey, though it has a very low rate of gun suicide. The National Police Agency of Japan has reported an increase in overall suicide from 1987 to 1988 of no less than 34% said to be due to the effects of the economic downturn in that country.19 Such a change can not be related to gun ownership levels.

REFERENCES

1. Cukier, Wendy. (1998), "Monument to the Victims" The Gazette (Montreal) 8th December.

2. United Nations Economic and Social Council, Commission on Crime Prevention and Criminal Justice, Criminal Justice Reform and Strengthening of Legal Institutions Measures to Regulate Firearms, Ref E /CN.15/1997/L, 25th April 1997.

3. Killias, Martin. (1993), "Gun Ownership, Suicide and Homicide: An International Perspective" in Understanding Crime: Experiences of Crime and Crime Control, del Frate, A; Svekic U; van Dijk, JJM; Eds. UNICRI Publication, No 49, Rome.

4. Sloan, J; Kellerman, A L; and Reay, D T; (1988), "Handgun Regulations, Crime, Assaults and Homicide: a Tale of Two Cities." *New England Journal of Medicine,* 319, 1256-62.

5. Newgreen, A, Chief Inspector of Police, (1987). "Report on Firearms Registration System", Victoria Police, Australia, 26th February

6. Private communication from The Shooting Sports Trust, Great Britain.

7. Greenwood, Colin, (1972), Firearms Control, A study of Armed Crime and Firearms Control in England and Wales, 235 - 239, London, Routledge & Kegan Paul Ltd.

8. (a) Morrison, S and O'Donnell, I. (1994) Armed Robbery, A Study in London, Oxford, University of Oxford Centre from Criminological Research (i) at 85, of 214 armed robbers only 16% received their first criminal conviction as a result of armed robbery. (99% were male). (ii) At 50, "None of the guns used by robbers were legally held by them. Indeed in most cases they would have been disqualified from holding a gun licence because of their previous criminal record."

(b) Home Office (1998), Criminal Statistics for England and Wales 1997, 203 London, Stationery Office. Only 26% of all male robbers (not merely armed robbers) had no previous convictions when convicted: 22% had ten or more previous convictions and the remainder had between 1 and 9 convictions.

(c) Kates, D.B. Lattimer, J.K. Boen, J.R. "Problematic Arguments for Banning Handguns." In Kates, DB. and Kleck G. (1997) The Great American Gun Debate, San Francisco, Pacific Research Institute for Public Policy. - "Innumerable criminological studies [show] murderers to be violent aberrants with extensive histories of felony, violence, mental imbalance, substance abuse and firearms and car accidents". (The studies are listed in the authors's notes.)

9. For some examples see The Home Office, (1998) *Criminal Statistics for England and Wales for 1997*, Chapter 10. London, The Stationery Office.

10. Clarke, R V and Mayhew, P. (1988) 'The British Gas Suicide Story and Its Criminological Implications'. In Crime and Justice: A Review of Research, Vol 10, University of Chicago Press.

11. Kleck, Professor Gary. (1997). Targeting Guns. Firearms and Their Control. 275 - 279. Aldine de Gruyter, New York.

12. Greenwood, Colin. (1972). *op cit,* 178 to 180.

13. Kleck, Professor Gary, *op cit* 97 where the author cites all sources for the figures.

14. Lott, John R. Jr. (1998). *More Guns Less Crime, Understanding Crime and Gun Control Laws.* 31. Chicago, University of Chicago

15. Kleck, Professor Gary, op cit 323 citing US Government statistics.

16. Home Office (1988). Home Office Statistical Bulletin 26.88 Firearm Certificate Statistics - England and Wales 1997.

17. Kleck, Professor Gary, *op cit* p 359.

18. Home Office (1996) Criminal Statistics for England and Wales 1995, Chapter 4. London, the Stationery Office.

19. Quoted in Coleman J Suicide Surge in Japan 3rd July 1999 issue of The Advertiser newspaper.

AUSTRALIA'S GUN CONTROL EXPERIMENT: A DECADE DOWN THE TRACK

Dr. Samara McPhedran and Dr. Jeanine Baker

After the 1996 mass killing of 35 people at the Port Arthur historical site, Australia enacted gun controls that are considered among the most stringent in the developed world. Briefly, the National Firearms Agreement (NFA), which was ratified by Federal Parliament in 1996 and implemented across all States and Territories by the end of 1997, prohibited certain types of firearms, in particular semi-automatic rifles and semi-automatic and pump action shotguns. To facilitate the removal of these firearms, a government funded 'buyback' scheme was designed, whereby owners were compensated for handing in their firearms. Over 640 000 firearms were subsequently destroyed by police, at an estimated cost to the taxpayer of AU$500 million (Australian National Audit Office, 1997). Compensation was not paid for illegal firearms, and very few were handed in.

The NFA also introduced strict requirements governing the possession of firearms, such as the necessity to have a proven or 'genuine reason' for firearm ownership (self defence was explicitly excluded), compulsory written safety tests, and the stipulation that all privately owned firearms must be registered through a State-controlled firearms licensing body. Additional components such as safe

Figure 1: Long term trends for firearm and non-firearm suicide in Australia

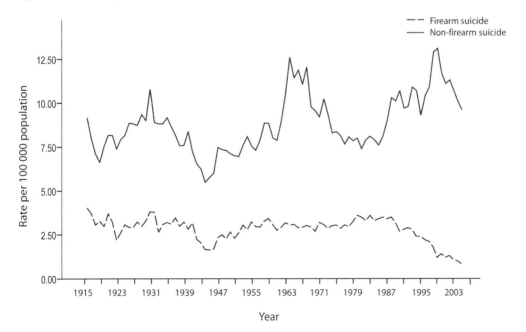

storage of firearms when not in use, and 28-day waiting periods for acquisitions of firearms were included in the reforms.

In the late 1990's research suggested that the NFA may have been successful in reducing firearm suicides, but ineffective for other firearm-related deaths (Carcach, Mouzos & Grabosky, 2002; Reuter & Mouzos, 2003). The effects of the reform remain contentious, particularly in regard to the useful-ness of the buyback of "low risk" firearms (Reuter & Mouzos, 2003) and in light of historical trends and notable declines in firearm suicide and homicide since the early 1980's (Figures 1 and 2).

Figure 2: Long term trends for firearm and non-firearm homicide in Australia

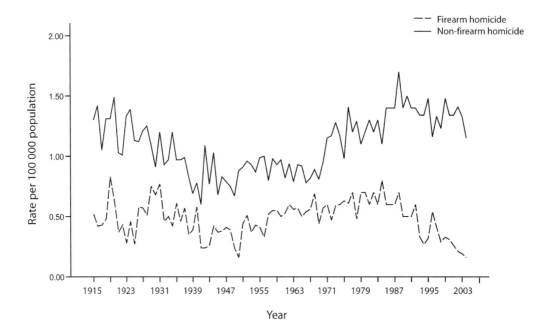

An increasing number of studies have set out to evaluate the impacts of the NFA on firearm-related deaths. Despite adopting disparate statistical approaches, extant studies on the impact of the NFA have produced consistent results. Baker and McPhedran (2007) found no significant difference in predicted and observed rates of firearm homicide post-1996 (that is, the pre-existing trend in fire-arm homicides did not accelerate). Independently replicating this finding, Chapman et al (2006) found no significant difference in trends for firearm homicide pre- and post-1996. Thus, it is now apparent that the tighter restrictions on ownership and the bans on civilian ownership of some types of firearms have not changed homicide trends in Australia.

Baker and McPhedran (2007) and Chapman et al (2006) showed a significant acceleration in the pre-existing downwards trend for firearm suicides – which account for around 80% of all firearm related deaths, and around 8% of all suicides in Australia – after the NFA was introduced. Baker and McPhedran (2007) and Chapman et al (2006) also discuss method substitution in relation to firearms legislation, and include non-firearm homicides and suicides in their analyses. Both studies agree that there is little evidence of method substitution post-1996, with non-firearm homicides and, particularly, non-firearm suicides also evidencing declines.

However, the decline in non-firearm suicides is noted by Baker and McPhedran (2007) as a confound when attempting to draw conclusions about the accelerated decline in firearm suicides post-1996 because it suggests other driving influences on suicide declines. The authors suggest that any effects of firearms legislation on firearm suicides cannot be adequately differentiated from the likely impacts of wider social changes (for example, improved funding for mental healthcare) on all suicides, regardless of method. The late 1990s saw the introduction of national suicide prevention strategies in Australia, which emphasised community awareness, destigmatisation of mental illness, and early intervention. Additionally, there has been an increase in the number of prescriptions provided for antidepressant medication (Hall, Mant, Mitchell, Rendle, Hickie, & McManus 2003).

Recent commentary extends these observations, suggesting that the legislative reforms do not appear to be responsible for declines in firearm suicide (De Leo, Klieve, & Barnes, 2008). Also, McPhedran & Baker (in press) have found that male non-firearm suicides in Australia declined more rapidly than male firearm suicides or female non-firearm suicides. This contradicts any claims that the NFA 'caused' the accelerated rate of decline in firearm suicide post-1996, because if this claim were true then firearm suicides would be expected to have fallen more rapidly relative to non-firearm suicides.

When the NFA was introduced, it was claimed by some legislators and gun control groups that increased safety training requirements would lead to declines in unintentional firearm deaths. Although the low number of unintentional firearm deaths in Australia each year and degree of variability from year to year highlights the need for caution when drawing any inferences about possible effects of the NFA, it is of interest that the downwards trend in unintentional firearm deaths pre-NFA did not continue post-reforms.

This observation may be a simple result of natural fluctuations in the data. However, an alternative explanation may lie with current data classification methods used by the Australian Bureau of Statistics (ABS). It has been suggested that ABS data 'under-counts' injury deaths, including suicides, and may 'over-count' unintentional deaths (De Leo, 2007). Until satisfactory resolution of potential data discrepancies arising from flawed counting methods can be achieved, claims that the stringent firearms legislation had an impact on firearm suicides or accidental deaths should be treated with due caution (McPhedran & Baker, 2008).

The 1996 reforms were introduced in reaction to the Port Arthur mass shooting, but it was stated at the time that the laws were intended to deliver a 'safer Australia', not to prevent future mass shootings (four or more fatalities) (Howard, 1996). Nonetheless, it has recently been argued that prevention of mass shootings has been achieved by the legislative changes (Chapman et al, 2006). However, this assertion has not been experimentally tested, due largely to the difficulties associated with statistical analysis of very rare events. More interestingly, it has been noted that New Zealand, like Australia, has not experienced a mass shooting in over a decade despite the continued legal availability in New Zealand of firearms now banned in Australia. This suggests that the absence of mass shooting events in Australia has more to do with the role of factors unrelated to legal firearms ownership, than with extravagant and untested claims about the legislative changes of 1996.

Despite the intensive media coverage and promises of greatly improved public health and safety made during the political campaign that accompanied the Port Arthur massacre of 1996, and the introduction of the NFA barely 2 weeks after the tragic event, it is now apparent that the costly legislation has not influenced trends in homicide or suicide in Australia. An unintended consequence of the NFA has, in fact, been to place substantial additional burdens on law enforcement officers and those approved to own firearms.

Regardless of its demonstrated failure to impact on the incidence of firearms abuse, the Australian experience with restrictive firearms legislation has been touted by some as a 'success', simply because the scheme removed a large number of legally owned firearms from civilians. However, this raises serious questions about whether the desired goal of firearms legislation is to reduce the abuse of firearms, or merely reduce the number of legally owned firearms without any concern for whether that approach will achieve genuine public health and safety outcomes. In the case of Australia, a decade down the track, it is clear that the 1996 gun control experiment has not delivered such outcomes. Therefore, the Australian NFA best serves as an expensive example to policy makers that if community safety is truly the goal, firearms legislation must take into account the sharp divide between legal use and criminal use, rather than mistakenly conflating the two.

References

Australian National Audit Office (1997). The gun buy-back scheme. Commonwealth of Australia, Australia Capital Territory.

Baker, J., & McPhedran, S. (2007). Gun laws and sudden death: Did the Australian firearms legislation of 1996 make a difference? *British Journal of Criminology* 47: 455-469.

Carcach, C., Mouzos, J., & Grabosky, P. (2002). The mass murder as quasi-experiment: The impact of the 1996 Port Arthur massacre. *Homicide Studies* 6: 109-127

Chapman, S., Alpers, P., Agho, K., & Jones, M. (2006). Australia's 1996 gun law reforms: faster falls in firearm deaths, firearm suicides, and a decade without mass shootings. *Injury Prevention* 12:365–372.

De Leo, D (2007). Suicide mortality data needs revision. *Medical Journal of Australia* 186(3): 157.

De Leo, D., Klieve, H., & Barnes, M. (2008). Australian firearms data require a cautious approach. *British Journal of Psychiatry* 191: 562-563.

Hall, W.D., Mant, A., Mitchell, P.B., Rendle, V.A., Hickie, I.B., & McManus, P. (2003). Association between antidepressant prescribing and suicide in Australia 1991-2000: Trend analysis. *British Medical Journal* 326: 1008-1012.

Howard, the Hon. J.W, Prime Minister of Australia (1996). Funding of gun 'buy back' scheme. Press Release, May 14.

McPhedran, S., & Baker, J. (2008). Australian firearms legislation and unintentional firearm deaths: A theoretical explanation for the absence of decline following the 1996 gun laws. *Public Health* 122: 297-299.

McPhedran, S., & Baker, J. (in press). Recent Australian suicide trends for males and females at the national level: has the rate of decline differed? Health Policy. doi: 10.1016/j.healthpol.2008.01.009

Reuter, P., & Mouzos, J. (2003). Australian gun control : assessing a massive buy-back of low risk gun groups. In P. Cook & J. Ludwig (eds.), *Evaluating gun policy: effects on crime and violence*. The Brookings Institute, Washington, pp. 121-142.

WOMEN AND GUNS: DOING IT FOR THEMSELVES

Mary Stange and Carol Oyster*

Feminism is surely in some ways responsible for the fact the women are increasingly choosing to take the responsibility for their own safety, and learning self-defense despite the fact that society remains reluctant to accept the legitimacy of women's taking lethal force power into their own hands. The large number of women who say they are taking steps to protect themselves are doing it out of a deep sense that their self-defense is worth fighting for. Rather than capitulating to the culture of male violence, these women are, as Naomi Wolf has suggested, fighting fire with fire.

As gun owner Leslita Williams, a middle-ages librarian, put it in an interview, "So much of nonviolent philosophy was dreamed up by men who didn't have to worry about the kinds of violence women face today. . . . Everyone has to decide for herself." William's own decision was based on the fact that in the mid-1980s a serial rapist was roaming her neighborhood in Athens, Georgia. She and seven of her friends, all of them "weaned on sixties-style nonviolence," enrolled in an armed self-defense course. They met together after each class, to talk over their feelings about the course and about guns. Ultimately, four of the women opted not to arm themselves, arguing that would amount to "stooping to the level of the enemy." Williams and three others decided that a pacifist approach was inadequate to the threat of a rapist-at-large; they bought handguns. Two things stand out about Williams's experience. One is that it clearly exemplifies that the choice to arm oneself can certainly arise from a commitment to feminist politics and practice; that is, from the conviction that women's lives, safety, and peace of mind matter, and that it is up to women themselves to take responsibility for their own well-being. The other is that these women, in deciding for or against firearms ownership, had made an informed choice.

Many Second Wave feminists continue to regard the violence inherent in the concept of armed or lethal force self-defense with a jaundiced eye. Like four of Williams's friends, they continue to take Audre Lorde's comment that the Master's tools cannot dismantle his house to mean that women must not embrace violence in any form. However, a new generation of feminists are beginning to think in different, almost revolutionary, terms about their relationship with violence.

One of them is Martha McCaughey. "I was once a frightened feminist," she remarks at the outset of her journey, both literal and theoretical, through the various options available to women for self-defense. As McCaughey experienced self-defense courses ranging from padded-attacker, martial arts, and cardio-combat to firearms use, she discovered that while "enacting an aggressive posture felt empowering, it [also] felt taboo—in my case doubly taboo as a woman and a feminist." But she also discovered that an enhanced sense of her aggressive physical power felt good. "Getting mean," she remarks, "is fun."

Research on the effects of women's self-protective skills on their self-image supports an idea of literal empowerment. After "Model Mugging" courses, women feel mare capable of defending themselves physically in the event of being attacked, which lead to a reduction in the number of limitations women place on their everyday activities. They now take risks with their behavior that would have been unthinkable before the training. McCaughey suggests: "If contemporary feminism has enabled the transformation of women's consciousness. And spawned a critique of the way the female body has been treated, represented, and thought of, self-defense training reveals how the traditional sexist ideas find their way into the functioning of the body itself. . . . Feminists have long considered the ways in which gender seems like biology but really isn't; self-defense illuminates the ways that gender is an ideology inseparable from, and alterable through, the lived body." Women who learn self-defense techniques not only see themselves and experience their bodies differently; they carry themselves differently, with more self-consciousness and self-confidence. Interestingly, believing you are safer can actually make you safer; rapists and muggers know how to read body language when selecting potential victims.

Yet because aggression is perceived as a male prerogative, women who become aggressive—even in the service of the own self-protection—risk being accused of "trying to be like men" and copping to patriarchal notions about power. McCaughey argues that "much feminist discourse has maintained a central assumption of bourgeois liberal individualism, namely that the body is an appendage of the self subjected to property rights. . . . This assumption turns the body into an object rather than an agent, thus rendering women's self-defense training irrelevant, inconsequential, or even antithetical to feminist politics." But accepting aggressive power as something of which women are and should be capable, far from being antithetical to feminism, creates a new "physical feminism." Women begin eagerly to accept their power to protect themselves from assailants, and will disrupt the societal "scripts" the define women as vulnerable victims and men as powerful and entitled.

McCaughey is not the only feminist to discover the liberating power of self-defense. Ellen Snortland encourages women to find the "warrior within" through physical self-defense training. Her book, Beauty Bites Beast: Awakening the Warrior within Women and Girls, avoids discussion of firearms, save for a brief mention in a question and answer appendix. When asked how one should respond to an attacker armed with a gun or a knife, she responds, puzzlingly: "One of the most potent aspects of learning full-force, full-contact self-defense is the ability the trained person has to talk to a potential assailant." Snortland does not explain the connection between a full contact self-defense course and the ability to converse, or how such a course would increase the ability. When asked about the wisdom of obtaining a gun instead of learning self-defense, as if the two were mutually exclusive, Snortland admits her anti-handgun bias. She suggests instead learning how to make weapons out of available household objects. But it is difficult to understand why this sound advice rules out using the most effective weapon available, a handgun, to break off an attack.

Certainly physical training for self defense is a good idea. It not only provides women with an opportunity for exercise and developing physical fitness, it also helps them develop a stronger sense of their own strength and agility. But basic size and strength differences between men and women cannot be denied. Many if not most women would not or could not train themselves to a level of proficiency that would make them truly equal to a man in hand to hand combat. And it is difficult to imagine any, except the most highly trained and physically fit among women, successfully fighting a man armed with a knife, bludgeon, or gun. Research has shown that a woman who forcefully resists stands a better chance of fending of an attacker than one who tries to talk her way out of the situation. However, the level of forceful resistance must be equivalent to the ferocity of the attack. And a handgun, as Arthur Kellermann himself acknowledged, is by far the most reliable self-defense against a potentially lethal attack.

Additionally, not all women are able to undertake physical self defense training. For older women and those with disabilities, a firearm may represent their only choice for active self protection. In each issue of its membership magazine American Guardian and American Rifleman, the NRA's "Armed Citizen" page features clippings from newspapers around the country, focusing on ordinary citizens' uses of firearms to thwart crime. Over the years an increasing number of these stories have been about women. The two following anecdotes are similar. These, however, were taken from a website on the internet on "Women and Self-protection."

> Geneva Littlefield, 61, and her 95-year old mother are quiet women who keep to themselves on their East Hall, Georgia, home. Geneva keeps a .38 cal. Revolver in case others don't do the same. After cutting the phone lines of the elderly women's home, a man broke in early one morning. Geneva heard him coming and was waiting for him. He began to choke her mother, so she shot him in the groin. Unable to call police and unwilling to leave her mother alone with the wound burglar, she held him at gunpoint until she could alert passing neighbors. (The Times, Gainesville, GA, 10/18/97)

> The burglar ransacked 81-year-old Alberta Nicles' Muskegon, Michigan, home before waking her up and ordering her around the house to search for money. Ending up back in her bedroom, the intruder—a suspected crack addict with a long history of criminal activity—removed the widow's pajama bottoms and was preparing to rape her when she informed him the she knew where there was some money. Her assailant let her up and followed her to a closet where the women instead retrieved her late husband's .38. She turned and shot her tormentor to death. Nicles then went to a neighbor's home to call police because her own line had been severed by the intruder prior to his breaking in. "This was not just a random breaking and entering. He was planning on taking advantage of the vulnerability of an elderly person. She was clearly acting in self-defense," Muskegon County Prosecutor Tony Tague said. (The Chronicle, Muskegon, Michigan, January 2, 1997)

In neither of these two cases would these women have been able to physically deter their attacker or protect themselves in any other way. One not uncommonly hears anti-gun feminists say they would rather die than own a gun. As these anecdotes demonstrate, that could represent a very real possibility.

Elderly and disabled women are not the only ones at a disadvantage when it comes to being able to actively defend themselves. As we have already had occasion to remark, generally anti-gun tenor of mainstream feminism reflects, and is to a large degree insulated by, a comfortably middle-class, white perspective. It is surely easier to forswear violent resistance if one belongs to a group that is statistically less likely to fall prey to violent attack. According to Bureau of Justice Statistics, Although women are one-third less likely to be victims of robbery or assault (excluding sexual assault) than men, certain women are far more vulnerable than others. These include women in the following risk categories: women aged 20-24 years; African-American women; divorced, separated, or single women; urban dwellers; women who never graduated from high school; and women who earn less than $10,000 a year. Women of color and poor women, many of whom share several of these risk factors, seldom have the luxury of debating about whether of not the Master's house can be dismantle using the Master's tools.

White liberals like to pontificate about the need to get "Saturday Night Specials" off the streets and out of the hands of criminals. The problem is, these relatively inexpensive handguns are generally not the ones involved in the commission of crimes; felons tend to steal, or to illegally buy on the black market, far more expensive sidearms. As law professor Robert Cottrol remarks: "Bans on firearms ownership in public housing, the constant effort to ban pistols poor people can afford—scornfully labeled 'Saturday night specials' and 'junk guns'—are denying the means of self-defense to entire communities in a failed attempt to disarm criminal predators. In many under-protected minority communities, citizens have been disarmed and left to the mercy of well-armed criminals."

And in these communities, a disproportionate number of households are headed by single women. If police will not protect them, they should at least have access to the tools with which they might protect themselves and their families.

THE RIGHT TOOL FOR THE JOB

A gun is simply a tool. Although anti-gun literature frequently treats firearms as if they were talismans, with magical powers of their own, the fact of the matter is that firearms in the home are dangerous only if used or stored irresponsibly. Guns can cave lives as well as take them. Bear in mind, in this connection, the defensive use of a firearm frequently does not require that it be discharged. Merely the threat or the sight of a firearm can terminate an attack. People, quite appropriately, fear handguns. Any felon will be the first to tell you this.

Research shows that the fact that the potential victims might be armed represents a risk for assailants that often affects, if, when, and where crime is committed. In one survey of over 1,500 incarcerated felons, over 80 percent agreed that smart criminals attempted to ascertain whether the intended victim is armed. More than half of the inmates reported they would change their target if they discovered, or even suspected, their original target was armed. Burglars reported that if they determined that a home was occupied they would avoid trying to break into the home because of specific fear of being shot. And perhaps most interesting of all more than half of the criminals reported being more concerned about running into an armed victim than into a police officer.

So a firearm can be a deterrent to crime by its mere presence. How many times a year are crimes thwarted or not committed for fear of an armed victim? As with the other statistics we have discussed in this chapter, this question is difficult to answer conclusively. As of 1995 at least fifteen surveys had attempted to measure the number of defensive gun uses each year. While it is relatively easy to obtain reliable statistics on actual crimes, it is extremely difficult to find solid data on crimes that weren't committed. The smallest estimate for the number of these defensive gun uses is 700,000 per year, but some others range higher.

The largest academic interview study of its kind, undertaken by criminologist Gary Kleck, found 2.5 million incidents of defensive handgun use in the United States between 1988 and 1993. Fifty-four percent of these uses were reported by women, which when multiplied by the population yields 1,180,586 defensive gun uses. This number may seem amazingly large, even to those who favor to armed self-defense, given the fact that there are no figures that would indicate that women own anywhere close to half of the firearms in our society. However, there is no mistake. Unlike other surveys that asked about gun use by any household member, this study specifically asked if the woman herself had used the gun. It's important to remember that in addition to between eleven and seventeen million women who own firearms themselves, far more have access to and experience with guns owned by other members of their households. It is equally important to remember that, as in case of sexual assault, surveys about gun use tend to be subject to a certain amount of underreporting. Kleck's work indicates that the civilian experience with defensive use of handguns appears to be approximately three times as common as the experience of victimization. The defensive value of the gun's mere presence is demonstrated by the study's finding that in only 8 percent of the 2.5 million defensive uses of guns, the firearm was actually fired.

If women are, in fact, responsible for over a million defensive uses of guns over a six-year period, who are these women? According to most studies, gun owners tend to be male, middle-aged, and relatively affluent. The women in one 1999 sample of firearms owners ranged in age ranged in age from 23 to 71. The median age was 48, which makes this sample comparable to previously reported samples of male gun owners. Household income ranged from $10,000 to $180,000, with a median of $55,000 for the combined household income. Only seven women reported incomes below $30,000, while eleven reported incomes over $100,000 per year. These relatively high incomes are likely related to the fact that half of the sample (sixty-one women) reported having completed college or an advanced degree. Not surprisingly, since the sample was composed of readers of firearms magazines, almost all (97 percent) own handguns. Over two-thirds of the sample bought their own handgun; 17 percent received their weapons as gifts.

The women were almost equally split between owing revolvers and semi-automatics pistols. Revolvers are the familiar "cowboy"-type of handgun where cartridges are loaded into a cylinder which advances each time the trigger is pulled. Semi-automatic handguns hold the cartridges in a magazine that is inserted into the grip of the gun; the firing of each round loads the next round into the chamber. For both types, only one bullet is fire by each pull of the trigger. The primary difference is that a larger number of bullets can be contained in a semi-automatic handgun. Gun women preferred a .38 caliber handgun, while men often prefer the heavier .45 caliber weapon. Four out five had undergone formal handgun training and described their skills as either intermediate or expert.

Over half of the women also own at least one rifle and at least one shotgun. However, for a variety of reasons, long guns are less effective as self-defense weapons the are handguns, so it is reasonable to assume they owned these gins for other purposes, like hunting and target shooting. When asked why they obtained a handgun, 60 percent of the women cited self-defense over competition, recreation, and hunting as their primary reason for handgun acquisition. This closely matches the reason given by men in a number if studies. These gun women generally were not responding to an incident or attack they had personally experienced, although 22 percent reported having been victims of serious crime. Most cited general concern for their personal safety. Of these women who reported using their handgun for self-defense (eighteen women representing 13 percent of the sample), only four had fires the weapon. As discussed earlier in regard to the deterrent value of firearms, most either displayed the weapon or informed the attacker they were armed.

Most of the sample (111 or 82 percent) reported carrying the handgun. Of this group, 40 percent (forty-four women) reported carrying the gun all time; an additional 43 percent (forty-eight women) reported carrying their gun when they expected to be in an unsafe environment. In other words, for most of these women, the handgun is an integral part of their daily routine. Unlike men who often carry their handguns in holsters, women reported various methods for carrying their guns, including purses of briefcases, purses or briefcases specially equipped with an internal holster, fanny packs, even diaper bags.

In terms of citizenship, this sample of gun women reported an unusually high level of civic involvement. Ninety-three percent were registered voters. Forty-six percent had written to a lawmaker in the past eight months, and an additional 13 percent had written both to a lawmaker and a letter to the editor. Thus, almost 60 percent were vocal in expressing their views and actively involving themselves in the democratic process.

Three out of four said they did not approve of gun control. Yet a small minority reported favoring waiting periods, mandatory firearms training for gun owners, banning certain types of weapons, and keeping gun out the hands of children (no more than twenty favored any type of control). It bears noting, regarding these responses, that there is a considerable disparity of opinion, among gun owners, regarding the phrase "gun control." Some interpret it to mean reasonable regulation, while others see it as in ordinate government intrusion into individuals' Second Amendment rights.

Both sides have a point. There is obviously a need for the lawful regulation of instruments as powerful as firearms, which helps to account for the fact that there are nationally over twenty thousand gun laws on the books. Indeed, some of the controls favored by some of the women are already federally mandated, including instant background checks (which in 1999 superseded the Brady law's waiting period), the prohibition of the sale of handguns to minors (as well as to convicted felons and persons deemed mentally incompetent), and the banning of certain models of guns that fall legislatively under the category of "assault weapons." Other controls vary by, and sometimes within, states. The most common argument cited by those who oppose gun control in any form is that the states and federal government should focus on strictly enforcing existing statues and punishing those who commit gun-related crimes to the full extent of the law, rather than further restricting the rights of the majority of gun owners who procured their guns legally and who abide by the law. Citing the cautionary adage, "When all arms are outlawed, only outlaw will be armed," some opponents of gun control further argue that the mare deeply the state intrudes onto individuals' decisions to keep or bear arms, the more likely individuals are to becoming de facto lawbreakers, by opting for legitimate firearms use even in the face of the law.

Whatever the validity of this latter argument, its force came through loud and clear in the survey. Asked "if it were illegal for you to carry a handgun for personal protection, and you felt threatened, would you carry anyway?" 86 percent (116 women) replied they would. It is, of course, a different matter to actually break a law than to report that you would hypothetically do so. A follow-up question therefore asked whether these women had actually broken the law by carrying illegally. Two-thirds reported that they had indeed carried illegally for the purpose of self-defense.

This sample presents an image very much in contrast to the stereotypes of gun owners. These women are well educated, relatively affluent, politically active, and responsible. Most carry handguns, apparently often illegally, for their own personal safety, even if it means taking their chances with the law. As several of the women stated, citing another cautionary adage: "it is far better to be judged by twelve, than to be carried by six."

WEIGHING THE RISKS

Advocates of restrictive gun control most commonly cite three reasons for limiting the availability of firearms: the potential for accidents; the use of the firearms in suicides; and the contention that the more guns there are in society, the higher the likelihood is that crime will occur. We have explored the potential positive effects of firearms ownership for women. Do these effects outweigh these three negatives? What do the statistics tell us about these problems?

The argument regarding accidents usually revolves around the question of children finding a gun and injuring themselves or someone else with it. Most reports of such gun-related accidents suggest that the firearm involved was stored in an irresponsible manner—that is, it was both accessible and loaded or with ammunition easily available—leaving open the question of whether these accidents occurred in the home of responsible firearms owners.

The NRA's Eddie Eagle program, nationally the most widely distributed gun safety program for children, emphasizes to children that if they happen upon a firearm unexpectedly they should stop, not touch the firearm, leave the room (or wherever the gun was), and immediately tell an adult. The police department of Lakewood, Colorado, in 1998 ran an experiment to determine whether children who have received the NRA's, or similar, firearm safety training would actually behave differently than who had never exposed to educational information about firearms. In a simulation involving a real though thoroughly disable gun, the children who had received training generally remembered and followed their training, leaving the room to report the presence of the firearm to an adult. Children who had not received safety training—who had been told, for example, only that "guns are bad"—were consistently more likely to approach and handle the firearm, even going so far as to aim it at themselves or another child. It would appear that failing to educate children on firearms safety in a society where approximately half the households contain firearms, rather than keeping these households safe, is more likely to render them scenes of accidents waiting to happen.

Using a more reasonable cut-off point of fourteen years old to describe children, the National Safety Council (figures for the year 1993, released in 1996) reports firearm-related accidents as a distant sixth cause of death, taking the lives of 205 children. The leading causes of accidental deaths in children include car accidents (3,044 deaths); drownings (1,023 deaths); fires and burns (1,015 deaths); mechanical suffocation (449 deaths); and ingestion of food or an object (223 deaths). The NSC figures suggest that a public health epidemiological approach would more appropriately be aimed at automobile and swimming pool safety than at firearms, since the combined deaths by auto and pool (4,067) represent almost twenty times the risk that firearms present to children. And approximately five million American homes have swimming pools, whereas an estimated 43 million households contain firearms. This is not to say that any child's accidental death by firearm is anything less that tragic. But it does put these tragedies, which almost invariably could have been prevented by the combination of gun safety education and a routine of responsible gun storage, into perspective. It also suggests that in the vast majority of households where there are both guns and children, gun owners are doing their part to keep firearms out of little hands.

What about suicide? Recall that of those forty-three deaths Kellermann attributed to the presence of a gun in the home, thirty-seven were suicides. Indeed, firearms are used more frequently for suicides than homicides. In 1993, gun deaths accounted for 48 percent of all suicides. Guns clearly represent a "serious" method of suicide highly likely to result in death, as compared to often "nonserious" methods such as ingestion of sleeping pills. However, increases in the number of available in American society do not relate in any systematic way to the number of suicides. Between 1972 and 1993 the number of guns per capita increased 54 percent. During this same time period the suicide rate was virtually flat—moving from 11.8 to 13 per 100,000.

The big question, of course, is if firearms were unavailable, could suicides be prevented? Perhaps. Another possibility is that the individual would simply choose another method. One of the research studies often cited by anti-gun physicians compares the cities of Seattle, Washington, and Vancouver, British Columbia, in terms of their accident and death rates. Although there are reasons of culture as well as laws controlling firearm availability (Canada has extremely restrictive firearm laws), the suicide rates for the two cities are virtually identical. The difference is in the method of suicide. As might be expected, very few of the suicides in Vancouver result from firearms. So although some in the psychiatric community argue that the suicidal are deterred if a firearm is unavailable (and it is the method of choice), at least in these two cities approximately equal numbers commit suicide; they simply do it differently.

Of course, cultural comparisons are always to some extent problematic. But the ready association between the presence of firearms and an increase likelihood of suicide is clearly refuted by the fact that in Japan, for example, where guns are a rarity, the suicide considerably higher than in the United States. In Israel, on the other hand, where virtually every household has one or more firearms, the rate is considerably lower. Switzerland, another heavily armed country, has a rate comparable to that of the U.S. Guns may facilitate suicide, but they do not cause it.

One factoid that made the rounds in the anti-gun press toward the end of the 1990s was that persons who purchase handguns are, within a few days of the purchase, at considerably higher risk if suicide than the general public. This ostensibly made waiting (or "cooling off") periods sound like a reasonable idea. But, as suicide researches have long affirmed, the fact is that people do not spontaneously decide to end their lives. Rather, the decision in favor of self-annihilation is arrived at over a period of time, and often in the context of clinical depression. The man or woman who purchases a handgun on Monday, and uses it to end his or her life on Tuesday, had already made that decision before walking up to the gun counter. The gun is the means, not the cause, and logically can hardly be considered a "risk factor"

Granted, on some level it is difficult to reduce the social and emotional cost of suicide to anything comprehensible by the term "logic." But the difficult fact remains that restricting access to handguns will not deter persons who are determined to end their lives. Some of these persons will be women. That, as appears to be the case, more women may be using guns to kill themselves than formerly is a bitter "down side" of changes occurring in American society. These changes, however, have to do with far more than women's increased gun ownership. In any event, argument that putting a gun in a woman's hand will turn her into a potential suicide is demeaning, trivializing, and insulting.

Do the number of guns available increase the likelihood of crime? This question needs to asked, if one is to decide whether guns are a public menace or a desirable option that some might reasonably choose for self-protection. The question became somewhat less murky in the late 1990s with the publication of research conducted by John Lott and David Mustard, first in a relatively inaccessible form (heavy on statistics in an academic journal), then in far more approachable style in Lott's book, More Guns, Less Crime.

Lott and Mustard analyzed data form the more than 3,000 counties in the United States for over twenty crime variables, over a period of fifteen years. These were further broken down on a number of demographic variables that included population, racial distribution, economic factors, crime rates, and, most importantly whether the state allowed concealed carry (for example, in a covered holster or in a purse) of firearms. The results of the study confirmed the intuitions of firearms owners and experts. Crime rates fell for violent crimes almost immediately after the passage of the concealed-carry laws and continued to drop over time. Presumably, this occurred in part because more citizens took advantage if their right to bear arms, in part because more criminals assumed they had. The average decreases were 7.7 percent for murder, 7.01 percent for aggravated assault, and 5.3 percent for rape.

The gains from these laws were not evenly distributed across all of the groups in the society. Lott observes some irony in this: "Women and blacks tend to be the strongest supporters of gun control, yet both obtain the largest benefits from nondiscretionary concealed-handgun laws in terms of reduced rates of murder and other crimes." Concealed carry changes the rules of the game of criminal victimization. As we have seen, when criminals know that their potential victim may be armed, that victim becomes a greater risk and far less appealing.

Perhaps the strongest example of the increases in safety that can be obtained from firearm ownership and responsible use can be illustrated by a program that was run by Orlando police department in 1966. The police trained 2,500 women in the defensive use of handguns. The program received a great deal of media attention, so potential criminals in the city were aware of the fact that any women they chose to target for victimization might be a trained gun women. The rate of rapes dropped by 88 percent in 1967 as compared to 1966, while the rate of rape in the rest of Florida remained at 1966 levels. Follow-up studies conducted five years later found the rate of rapes still 13 percent below the preprogram rate in Orlando. In the surrounding areas, however, the rate had increased 300 percent in the intervening five years.

The evidence is clear that in the hands of untrained or irresponsible people, firearms can represent a hazard to life and limb. For those individuals who train themselves and follow safety rules, however, firearms can offer not merely a sense of increased safety, but an actual avenue to increased safety. And this maybe especially true for women. Feminism at its best represents the opportunities for individuals to make choices: about the careers, about their life-style, and about reproductive rights. Not everyone will make the same choice to protect herself with a firearm should be equally respect. And for today's gun women, whether they call themselves feminists or not, armed self-protection is a responsibility they are willing to assume.

SMALL ARMS SURVEY: A CRITIQUE

A CRITIQUE OF METHODS USED TO ESTIMATE CIVILIAN FIREARMS IN *SMALL ARMS SURVEY 2007, GUNS AND THE CITY*

Gary Mauser[1]

In this essay I briefly criticize the methodology used in the recent publication, S*mall Arms Survey 2007, Guns and the City,* to estimate global firearm stock. My critique will focus exclusively on Chapter 2, "Completing the Count, Civilian Firearms", by Aaron Karn, which introduces important modifications to previous approaches used by the Small Arms Survey (SAS) group for estimating firearm stock (Killias, 1993; SAS 2002, 2006). The principal innovation in Chapter 2 is a new way to estimate the number of firearms held outside of national governments, referred to here as "civilian firearms". Using this new approach, the SAS estimates have nearly doubled for world-wide firearm stock, jumping to 875 million from 500 million. This increase is only apparent, as it is due entirely to changing methods for estimating non-governmental firearms. The author asserts that 650 million of these firearms are held outside of government (by "civilians"). It is important to assess this new, and supposedly more sophisticated, approach in order to evaluate its contribution.

The first point to consider is the doubtful utility of firearms stock as an explanatory variable. No empirical justification is offered, so it is somewhat surprising to discover that the author of this chapter merely assumes that firearms ownership, and particularly civilian firearms ownership, is the driving force behind civil unrest and criminal violence internationally.

There is very little explanatory power in such a simplistic measure as firearms stock. Over the past few decades, academic researchers, political scientists as well as economists, have studied a wide variety of factors that theoretically may contribute to intra-national and inter-national conflict. A few of the more important factors are: lack of economic freedom, income disparity, poverty, slow economic growth, organized crime, non-democratic government, governmental corruption, low adult-education levels, drug trafficking, and a history of violent ethnic conflict. Scholars have empirically evaluated these variables in a wide variety of studies, but little evidence has emerged that would suggest that firearms stock or civilian firearm ownership are important contributory factors (Azar and Burton, 1986; Deering and Pollins, 2003; Rummel, 1981, 1998; United Nations, 2007; Zartman, 2000).

Interestingly, the author appears to want to have it both ways. In the introduction, the author asserts that the availability of firearms is equated with social problems, even depravity: "Many of the examples in this chapter illustrate a strong connection between ownership levels and depravity." At the same time, he readily admits that " 'gun cultures' do not automatically translate into armed conflict" (both on p. 40). One might reasonably ask: if firearms are only occasionally associated with social problems, does it not follow that other factors may well be more important? No empirical evidence is presented in this chapter that demonstrates a link between lawful civilian firearms ownership and social problems.

Later in the chapter, the author admits that "gun ownership is highly concentrated among the largest and wealthiest societies". Table 2.3 shows the countries that the author estimates to have the largest holdings of firearms. Many of these are among the most politically stable countries in the world and are able to boast of admirable histories of low levels of violence[2]. Thus the very data presented in Chapter 2 undermine their author's claim that civilian firearm ownership contributes to social chaos, violent crime or armed conflict. Moreover, analyses of other data collected by the Small Arms Survey, for other subsets of countries, fail to conform to their assumption that civilian firearm ownership is linked to criminal or political violence (Kates and Mauser 2007; Kopel, et al, 2003; Mauser 2005).

CONCEPTUAL PROBLEMS

Conceptual confusion abounds in Chapter 2. The author frequently moves back and forth between terms such as, 'criminal violence', 'gun violence', 'gun crime', 'armed conflict' and 'social chaos'. The result is to equate violence involving firearms with civil unrest or criminal violence. This is confusing because firearm-related violence is only a fraction of total criminal violence. In politically stable countries, violent crime involving firearms is typically a very small portion of total criminal violence. For example, in Canada firearms were used against a victim in just 2.4 percent of all criminal violence in 2006 (Dauvergne, and De Socio, 2007). Nor are firearms the primary weapons involved in countries torn by civil strife or insurrectionary violence. In Rwanda, for example, machetes were used to murder almost all of an estimated 800,000 people in 1994. Firearms were not widely available to the killers, although the government did distribute grenades, and to a lesser extent, firearms, to select groups of their supporters (Human Rights Watch, 2008). Such intellectual sloppiness on the part of the author obscures real differences in the types of violence that threaten civil society, e.g., criminal activity or insurrectionary violence. The result is that the threat of firearms is greatly exaggerated.

Additional conceptual problems mar the chapter. In analysing the potential threat of firearms, it is important to distinguish basic types of firearms and firearm owners. This is not done. Surprisingly, the author uses the term "firearm" to include a wide variety of things that are not firearms[3]. The author's treatment of firearms owners is equally egregious. While ignoring definitions, he initially recognizes three distinct types of firearm owners: governments, civilians, and criminals. Despite recognizing the difference between civilians and criminals, and presumably terrorists and revolutionaries, the author quickly subsumes them all into a vague general category, "private ownership", which he then labels "civilians". This is overly simplistic and misleading.

By treating criminals as equivalent to responsible citizens who obey laws surrounding gun ownership, the author, perhaps inadvertently, violates not only common sense but also the basic assumptions that underlie democratic governments around the world. This approach abandons any pretense that governments derive their legitimacy from popular sovereignty. If there are no real differences between criminals and responsible citizens, then democratic government is no different from dictatorship. Indeed, the author implies that governments have no duty to be responsible to their citizens. In taking this approach he undermines the legitimacy of modern democratic governments.

On a more practical and immediate level, by not differentiating between responsible civilians and criminals, the author confuses the problems in estimating firearm numbers for each of these categories. (This point will be expanded on in the next section). There is a great deal of information published about legal firearms that is not available for illegal firearms. Finally, this confusion unnecessarily exaggerates the potential threat of longstanding civilian firearms ownership within any given country.

The analysis in this chapter errs in still another way. In evaluating the threat of firearms, the author simplistically ignores important differences amongst countries. The justification offered for glossing over this is that the focus is merely to gain a count of the number of firearms. This is disingenuous because accuracy in counting of firearms would be facilitated if he recognized important national differences. More and better data (e.g., surveys, official records) are available for wealthier and more democratic countries but not for many others. Moreover, in all likelihood differences among countries have much more to do with the potential of violence and social chaos than the mere number of firearms in a country.

The author merely assumes there is a greater danger in privately owned firearms than firearms possessed by a government, although he does not provide any support for such a belief. It would appear obvious that the potential threat of a government depends critically upon the nature of the government in question. Some governments (e.g., North Korea, the former USSR, or Zimbabwe) undoubtedly pose larger threats to their citizens than do more democratic governments (e.g., France, Canada, or New Zealand). Unfortunately, the author appears oblivious to this important observation, for in his discussion of the threat posed by firearms, he makes no serious attempt to evaluate or even in passing to identify differences among national governments around the world.

METHODOLOGICAL PROBLEMS

The author reports that he used three different approaches to estimate private firearms stock in 178 countries. The first relies upon the firearm registry in a country, the second utilizes so-called "independent" estimates made by experts or informants selected by the author, and the third uses a simple statistical model. Despite the scanty description of these approaches, I will attempt to briefly evaluate them. The bulk of the claims for countries included in this chapter are derived from these "independent estimates". Unfortunately, none of the estimating approaches used here are described sufficiently to be able to adequately evaluate them.

The author, quite properly in my judgment, employs a variety of approaches to estimate firearm stocks. However, instead of presenting and evaluating each of these approaches separately, the author jumbles them all together, mixing countries and approaches together seemingly at random. This violates accepted practice. When multiple estimation methods are employed, each one should be evaluated separately and accompanied by individual error analyses. Beyond painting his problems and solutions with very broad brushstrokes, the author provides no empirical support for his claims of accuracy for any of the methods he employs. [4]

It is exceptionally challenging to estimate the number of firearms because of the sensitive nature of this inquiry and the intrinsic importance of firearms to both owners and governments. All gun owners – governments, civilians, criminals and insurrectionary forces – have clear reasons for being less than candid about firearm ownership. This reluctance can be found both in survey studies and in official records. These challenges necessitate, as the author recognizes, deploying multiple methods that rely upon different types of data. Used properly, multiple methods allow for cross checking. Unfortunately, the author fails to adequately present empirical support for his claims.

One of the hallmarks of responsible research is the open reporting of methodology. Openness allows readers to decide for themselves the validity of the findings, and it allows others to attempt to reproduce the findings from the data. Criminological phenomena are complex. Anyone who ventures into the minefields of estimating such phenomena, including estimating the numbers of weapons, is rudely introduced to the inherent challenges of the undertaking. While the author allows that he encountered difficulties in making these estimates, he is not more specific in admitting what they were or what limitations were thereby imposed. Instead, he incongruously stresses the validity of the approach.

Firearm registration

The author is quite correct in believing that firearm registration records do not include all firearms within a country. This is certainly true even for the most modern and technologically advanced countries for a variety of reasons. It would be unreasonable to expect that criminals would register their firearms. In addition, many countries exempt their own military, as well as other classes of governmental firearms, from the civilian registry. Thus, even for the 52 countries that the author believes have solid and reliable firearm registries, the author quite legitimately relies upon independent estimates for substantial contributions to his estimate of total civilian firearms stock in a country. Another 25 countries, according to the author, have firearm registration, but he does not trust the data, preferring to rely upon independent estimates[5]. No firearm registry data are available for another set of 25 countries. Here his estimates are based solely upon his so-called "independent estimates".

Independent estimates

Given the importance of so-called "independent estimates" in the determination of privately held (or non-governmental) firearm stock, that is, what the author refers to as "civilian" firearms, it is especially disappointing that the author does not provide adequate information to allow the approach to be evaluated. He says he carefully weighed the various estimates made for each country. Yet, with a few exceptions, he does not provide any details about the independence or the quality of the estimates. Evaluating the quality is crucial. It is important to know who these estimators were; how they were selected; how many separate estimates were used in determining the number of firearms in each country; and exactly how conflicting estimates were resolved. We are not told. Despite using sophisticated language, the author does not make clear how these "independent estimates" differ substantially from the previous methods which the author scorns as "unsophisticated" since they are merely "indirect techniques" or worse, generated from "a sense of feel". The details that might demonstrate the superiority of the author's approach remains unavailable in the yet-to-be-published annexes.

Statistical modelling

The author uses a simple statistical model to estimate the number of firearms in the remaining 76 countries. Despite the implications that this model is based upon more than one basic national indicator, I could find only one, the GDP per capita. Apparently, this model is a simple bivariate linear regression between GDP per capita and the estimated non-governmental firearms stock. The author's description is vague and incomplete. It is not clear whether one world-wide model was used to estimate civilian firearms stock, or regional models were used. And if regional models, it is unstated how many were involved. Nor is it clear how many countries the author used as the base for his model. Was the model developed on the 52 countries where the author had the best estimates, or were all 102 countries included where estimates of any quality were made? Whichever is the case, the author calculates a linear relation between GDP per capita and his estimates of gun ownership using his base, and then he predicts from their GDP per capita the number of firearms civilians own in individual countries. This is not a very sophisticated model, and merely results in the non-threatening and totally unsurprising discovery that civilians in the richer and more stable countries in the world have more firearms than do non-state actors in the poorer and less stable countries.

SUMMARY

This paper reviewed the methodology used in, "Completing the Count, Civilian Firearms," *Small Arms Survey 2007, Guns and the City*, to estimate the number of firearms held outside of national governments. The principal innovations consist of so-called "independent estimates" and a simple regression model.

Conceptual confusion riddles this chapter and exaggerates the threat of civilian firearms ownership. The author conflates responsible firearms owners with criminals, revolutionaries and terrorists, who are together referred to as "civilians". Gun violence, even though it is but a fraction of total violent crime, is treated as synonymous with violent crime and civil unrest. The term "firearm" is mistakenly used to include objects other than firearms.

The firearms count relies upon "independent estimates" that are not described in a fashion sufficient to allow evaluation. Despite their critical nature, no systematic attempt is made to justify the qualifications of the people making these estimates. The author claims that important information is to be found in the annexes, which however remain unpublished.

The author merely assumes his conclusions. He uses a simple linear model to estimate the number of firearms held outside of government uniquely from the wealth of a country. This simplistic model merely reaches the obvious and non-threatening prediction that individuals in richer countries have more firearms. This result contradicts the author's claims about the threats posed by "civilian" firearms ownership because richer countries tend to be more politically stable and to have less civil unrest.

References

Azar, Edward and John Burton. (eds.) *International Conflict Resolution: Theory and Practice,* Boulder, Colorado: Lynne Rienner Publishers, 1986.

Dauvergne, Mia and Leonardo De Socio (2007). "Firearms and Violent Crime", *Juristat,* Vol 28, No 2, Statistics Canada.

Human Rights Watch. "Leave None to Tell the Story: Genocide in Rwanda", *Human Rights Watch,* Report http://www.hrw.org/reports/1999/rwanda/ (Updated 1 April 2004) [from wikipedia, Rwanda.]

Jane's Information Services. http://www.janes.com/press/press/pc080326_1.shtml

Kates, Don B., Gary Mauser. "Would Banning Firearms Reduce Murder and Suicide? A Review of International and some Domestic Evidence", *Harvard Journal of Law and Public Policy*, Spring 2007, Vol. 30, No 2, pp 650-694.

Killias Martin. "International correlations between gun ownership and rates of homicide and suicide", *Canadian Medical Association Journal*, Vol. 148, No 10, October 1993, pp. 429-48.

Kopel, David, Paul Gallant and Joanne Eisen. "Gun Ownership and Human Rights", *Brown Journal of World Affairs*, Vol 9, Winter/Spring 2003.

Mansfield, Edward Deering and Brian M. Pollins (eds.) *Economic Interdependence and International Conflict: New Perspectives on an Enduring Debate* (Michigan Studies in International Political Economy), University of Michigan Press, 2003

Mauser, Gary. "'Trouble in Paradise: Small Arms in the Pacific': A Brief Critique", a paper prepared for The Guns Summit, 4-8 July 2005, University of Goroka, Papua New Guinea, July 2005.

Rummel, RJ. *Power Kills*, Transaction Publishers, Brunswick, NJ, 1998.

Rummel, RJ. *Understanding Conflict and War*, Sage Publications, Beverly Hills, CA. 1981

Small Arms Survey 2002. *Small Arms Survey 2002, Counting the Cost*, Oxford, Oxford University Press, 2002.

Small Arms Survey 2006. *Small Arms Survey 2006, Unfinished Business,* Oxford, Oxford University Press, 2006.

Small Arms Survey 2007. *Small Arms Survey 2007, Guns and the City,* 2007, Cambridge University, UK.

United Nations Office on Drugs and Crime. *Crime Violence, and Development: Trends, Costs and Policy Options in the Caribbean.* Report 37820. Vienna, Austria. March, 2007.

Zartman, I. W. (2000). Ripeness: The hurting stalemate and beyond. In P. C. Stern & D. Druckman (Eds.), *International conflict resolution after the Cold War.* Washington, DC: National Academy Press.

Endnotes

1. Gary Mauser is Professor Emeritus, Simon Fraser University, Burnaby, BC, Canada.

2. In fact, 11 of the countries identified as having the largest civilian holdings of firearms are included in the list of 50 most secure countries in the world that was recently released by Jane's Information Services (2008). As well, this list somehow fails to include the 10 least stable countries in the world (Gaza, Somalia, Afghanistan, Sudan, Cote d'Ivoire, Haiti, Zimbabwe, Chad, Democratic Republic of Congo, and the Central African Republic), also identified by Jane's (2008).

3. Some examples illustrate this confusion. Starter pistols (which cannot shoot projectiles) are included in his analysis of firearms in the United Kingdom; in a later section, he includes a wide variety of military weapons, such as mortars and grenades, as if they were firearms.

4. The annexes in which the methodology is supposedly described more fully are still not available more than one year after publication. Such failure to publish annexes and methodological details has also occurred in earlier SAS publications.

5. Many countries, such as South Africa, simply lack the technical infrastructure to adequately maintain a firearm registry.

UNITED NATIONS GLOBAL INITIATIVES: FIREARMS PROTOCOLS

THE UN'S GLOBAL EFFORT TO DISARM CIVILIANS: WISDOM OR FOLLY?

Joyce Lee Malcolm*

> **"Everyone has the right to life, liberty and security of person."**
> **-The Universal Declaration of Human Rights, United Nations**

American and UN weapons inspectors may have failed to find weapons of mass destruction in Iraq, but in April 2003 Kuniko Inoguchi, Japan's ambassador to the UN Conference on Disarmament, informed a 20-nation conference at Oslo that she had found them everywhere. Inoguchi's weapons of mass destruction are "small arms"— a category the conference referenced as including everything from handguns to shoulder-fired anti-tank weapons.[1] These have been dubbed de facto WMD because, at UN reckoning, they kill 57 people an hour and at least 500,000 people a year.[2] Of this number, 300,000 deaths are estimated to occur in military conflicts, the remaining 200,000 in civilian murders, accidents or suicides." As if creating all this mayhem were not bad enough, Inoguchi and her colleagues point out that "illicit trafficking" in small arms "is linked to other kinds of trade, in drugs, human beings …it's linked to all types of criminal organizations and to terrorism." Inoguchi went on to chair the Vienna-based Conference on Disarmament, an institution dedicated to implementing the UN's 2001 Firearms Protocol, a global action plan passed by the General Assembly to outlaw trafficking in weapons ranging from machine guns to pistols.[3] By 2003, sixteen nations had signed on to the plan, and the European Union is expected to ratify it shortly.

THE CAMPAIGN FOR A GLOBAL SMALL ARMS TREATY

It is only recently that those aiming to control small arms have taken to referring to them as weapons of mass destruction, but the global campaign to curb "trafficking" in small arms is now ten years old and counting. With the collapse of the Cold War, much arms control effort has been diverted from nuclear to conventional weapons — weapons ranging from military equipment right down to the pistol on the bedside table. The goal is far more ambitious than merely curbing illicit international trade in small arms, or even illicit national trade, ambitious as those aims are. The agenda of the various UN agencies and the international NGOs working with them is to pass an international treaty to control possession of small arms throughout the world, both between and within nations. In the process, the treaty would, by determining what is illicit, of necessity determine which individuals, groups and entities should be trusted to be armed.4

Child soldier in Sierra Leone.

Although the numbers of military and civilian deaths from small arms are lumped together, much of the real focus is on privately-owned weapons, and not merely those in the hands of criminals and terrorists, but those belonging to law-abiding civilians. The Executive Director of the UN Office for Drug Control and Crime Prevention, Pino Arlachhi, reminded delegates at a UN workshop on small arms and crime in New Delhi, that they were to deal with "problems with civilian-owned firearms." One of four such regional workshops, its agenda included "the link between firearm availability and crime," firearm-related homicides, suicides and accidents and national practices "relevant to firearm regulation."5 The 1995 UN Crime Congress, alarmed that "small, illegally owned firearms were killing more people than major weapons," had urged the UN Centre for International Crime Prevention to take up the issue of civilian-owned firearms. The Crime Congress was also parent to the first-ever international survey of firearms ownership and regulation. A preliminary report was published in Vienna in 1997.

Coming from these two directions, disarmament and crime, the UN has sponsored regular biennial meetings since 1995 to monitor progress on a small arms agreement and hosted a series of regional meetings around the world to further that agenda. Reports and recommendations have been duly produced. A 16-member panel of experts appointed by the UN Secretary-General and chaired by ambassador Mitsuro Donowaki of Japan, produced a 37-page report in 1998 that, according to Ambassador Donowaki, contained "the best available wisdom of our times." It urged that steps be taken to reduce and prevent problems caused by accumulations of small arms. A UN conference in New York in 2001 produced a "Programme of Action."6 The huge document's cautious approach disappointed many proponents with its failure to address transfers to non-state actors, restrictions on "civilian possession."7

Worries about civilian owned firearms have also been echoed by regional groups. In January 2005 under the headline, "Millions of Small Arms in Civilian Hands Pose a Danger to Public Security," the Gambia Daily News reported that sub-Saharan Africa had some 30 million "small arms and light weapons," of which 79 per cent were in the hands of civilians, 19 percent with the police and military and 2 percent with the insurgents.8 Gambia's permanent secretary at the Department of State for Defence described the situation as "potentially dangerous" and looked forward to collaborating fully with the new small arms control program of the Economic Community of Western African States (ECOWAS).

East African states have already acted. In April 2004, eleven East African nations signed the Nairobi Firearms Protocol. Its contents reveal the sorts of measures the small arms controllers are advocating:

- a ban on civilian ownership of automatic and semi-automatic rifles

- registration of all guns

- regulation of gun storage and competency testing for prospective owners

- restrictions on the number of guns a person can own

- a ban on pawning of guns

- uniform minimum standards regulating manufacture, control, possession of small arms

- uniform tough sentencing for unlicensed gun possession 9

Running some guns in Sadr City, Iraq.

These restrictions will reduce, and could eliminate, the ability of law-abiding citizens of these countries to be armed, while doing nothing to restrict or reduce the weapons in the hands of their military or police. South Africa's new gun licensing law, for example, is being used to reduce drastically the number of guns in private hands, leaving thousands of people, many living in areas where the police are unable to protect them, unable to protect themselves.10 Andrew Soutar, chairman of the South African Arms and Ammunition Dealers Association, complained: "Not a single license has been issued for a firearm that the association is aware of."11 In Botswana, the government will only process 400 applications for guns each year. The successful applicants are chosen by lottery.12

Are the governments that will be the signatories to the hoped-for global treaty to be trusted not to harm their citizens once they, their armies and police, have a monopoly on weapons?

NON-GOVERNMENTAL ORGANIZATIONS AND SMALL ARMS

International non-governmental organizations, buoyed up by their great success in the drafting and passage of the 1997 Ottawa Convention to Ban Antipersonnel Land-mines, have been deeply involved in these UN meetings and conferences—200 NGOs attended the July 2001 UN "Conference on the Illicit Trade in Small Arms and Light Weapons in All Its Aspects"—and are busy with their own campaigns to promote civilian disarmament. In December 2004 the Million Faces Petition was unveiled in Tokyo.13 Makoto Teranaka, secretary general of Amnesty International Japan, one of the organizers, explained that this "visual petition" of photos is intended to show "concern about the proliferation and misuse of arms around the world and urge governments to take action on tougher arms control."14 It is to be presented to world leaders in July 2006 when a UN conference on small arms convenes.

The petition is part of the Control Arms campaign launched in October 2003 by Amnesty International, Oxfam International, and The International Action Network on Small Arms (IANSA), a global campaign "to curb rampant use" of small arms.15 Amnesty International Japan is leading the campaign in Japan with four other groups: Oxfam Japan, Network Earth Village, Terra Renaissance and InterBand Network Earth Village. The latter two are members of IANSA. By late December 2004 the Million Faces Petitions had 209,564 signatories, including photos of celebrities such as film director Michael Moore.16

* * *

Every right-thinking individual deplores deaths in warfare or from criminal violence, whether caused by so-called small arms or by any other means. And certainly there are civilians who misuse guns. But in their zeal to institute world-wide small arms controls, proponents of the campaign are ignoring important issues, indeed the most basic issues. The first question should be whether the strict control, and perhaps complete removal, of the law-abiding citizen's access to firearms is the best, or even a good way, to reduce violence against civilians. Are the governments that will be the signatories to the hoped-for global treaty to be trusted not to harm their citizens once they, their armies and police, have a monopoly on weapons? Is access to firearms for personal protection necessary, or would the public be safer without it? Article 51 of the Charter of the United Nations insists that "Nothing in the present Charter shall impair the inherent right of individual or collective self-defense if an armed attack occurs against a Member of the United Nations." Should the UN apply different standards to the people it is meant to protect than it does to the governments that are its members?

SMALL ARMS DEATHS: STATISTICS AND DEFINITIONS

Before we turn to these questions, it is worth briefly examining the basis for the number of small arms victims, some 500,000 annually, cited repeatedly by the UN and NGOs active in the arms control campaign. In a painstaking analysis, David B. Kopel, Paul Gallant and Joanne D. Eisen found the toll of 500,000 killed by small arms annually, 300,000 in military conflicts, 200,000 in homicides, suicides and accidents, a wild exaggeration of the number of both military and non-military deaths.17 The figure for war deaths assumes that all military fatalities are from small arms and light weapons. The actual figure for military deaths from firearms is closer to 115,000 than to 300,000.18

There is also a scrambling of categories of weapons. The Small Arms Survey defines "small arms" as revolvers and self-loading pistols, rifles and carbines, assault rifles, sub-machine guns and light machine guns. It defines "light weapons" as "heavy machine guns, hand-held under-barrel and mounted grenade launchers, portable anti-tank guns, anti-aircraft missile systems" and some mortars. The UN refers to small arms as "weapons designed for personal use."19 But the small arm label is often stretched to include both personal small arms and military light arms.20 The authors of the Small Arms Survey

2002 admit that this issue was deliberately avoided at the 2001 UN Small Arms Conference. They concede the Small Arms Survey, "uses the terms `small arms,' `firearms,' and `weapons' interchangeably. Unless the context dictates otherwise, no distinction is intended between commercial firearms (e.g. hunting rifles) and small arms and light weapons designed for military use (e.g.assault rifles)."21 This approach of mixing weapon types, then focusing exclusively on small arms, was the practice from early in the campaign. In his "Prologue" to the 1997 report of the Secretary General's Advisory Board on Disarmament Matters, Mitsuro Donowaki referred to the "proliferation of small arms and light weapons," moved on to "small arms made to military specifications" and the "widespread proliferation of light weapons" that victimized millions of civilians and had led the UN General Assembly to request a report, not on light weapons, or "military style small arms," but "on ways and means to deal with the particular dangers and challenges posed by small arms."22 The report was placed on the UN agenda as "General and Complete Disarmament: Small Arms,"23

Weapons confiscated from the Muqtada Militia in Najaf, Iraq.

As for civilian-caused firearms fatalities, the UN's figure of 200,000 annually is also dubious. The World Report on Violence and Health (2002), the latest data on the subject, found 44,862 firearm-related homicides annually, based on the 45 countries that had good records on the subject. But the WHO could not explain how it arrived at its final figure of 200,000 firearms deaths in peaceful countries. As Kopel, Gallant and Eisen note, since the 45 countries the WHO has used include those with the highest rates of civilian firearms ownership, it seems unreasonable that countries whose citizens own only a tiny proportion of civilian-owned firearms would account for over three times as many non-war firearms deaths as the countries possessing the great majority of civilian firearms.

Further, some 57.1 percent of the civilian firearms deaths reported by the WHO were suicides. Including these deaths assumes the suicides would not have occurred had firearms not been available, a doubtful assumption. An editorial in the British Medical Journal found that given the absence of one means of suicide, someone wanting to take his own life will simply use another.24 A comparison of the American and Japanese rates of suicide illustrates the relative unimportance of firearms as a factor in suicide. Japan boasts the strictest gun control of any democracy, while Americans own an estimated 200 million firearms. Yet the overall Japanese suicide rate is nearly twice as high as the American rate.25

Combined military and non-military deaths from small arms are probably less than 200,000.26 While far less than the much-touted 500,000 fatalities, the more accurate figure, of which some 80,000 are non-military casualties, is still a very serious toll. The question is whether a global treaty restricting civilian access to firearms would reduce or increase it.

IS A GOVERNMENT MONOPOLY OF SMALL ARMS WISE?

Proponents of a global small arms treaty assume it is civilian ownership of firearms that threatens ordinary people. A brief examination of the past century, however, reveals that, on average for each year of the 20th century, governments took at least 20 times more lives than civilian gun murderers.27 The calculation is simple. If you assume an average of some 80,000 civilian-perpetrated murders per year world-wide, there would been some eight million ordinary gun 30 murders for the century.28 However, as Don B. Kates points out in his essay, "Human Rights and Genocide—the Misguided International Public Health Effort to Disarm Civilian Populations," individuals acting for governments—military, police, groups armed by governments—murdered over 170 million non-combatant civilians during the 20th century. This number does not include accidental civilian deaths in wars. Rather than diminishing that appalling figure, disarming civilians may actually increase government-perpetrated murders by removing a basic deterrent to state-sponsored violence.

Governments intent on terrorizing or slaughtering specific groups of citizens nearly always take the precaution of disarming their intended victims first. The most notorious case is the Holocaust, where the Nazis disarmed Jews before launching their "final solution."29 But there have been many other examples. The Khmer Rouge, after taking power in Cambodia, conducted a house-to-house search for

Not a Yankees rally.

weapons through-out the country. As one witness reported, they would knock on the door and ask the people inside if they had any weapons. "We are here now to protect you," the soldiers said, "and no one has a need for a weapon any more." Even when people replied that they had no weapons, their huts were searched. Once the soldiers felt sure the have people had no weapons, the killing began. 30 With the people disarmed, the 100,000 member Khmer Rouge army was able to kill some 2.5 million Cambodians. The 30,000 men of Idi Amin's death squads slaughtered 300,000 unarmed Ugandans. In testimony before the UN Human Rights Commission in Geneva, 2003, Kates also cited government violence against unarmed civilians in the war between Ethiopians and Eritreans when Eritrea seceded. To terrorize the citizens of the breakaway region, Ethiopia's army exterminated 300,000 unarmed Eritreans. Then there are the massacres carried out by the Serbian government during the 1990s. The well-armed Serbs attacked the Bosnian Muslims, who were unarmed and unable to get weapons to defend themselves because of a UN embargo. The UN had told the Bosnian Muslims they didn't need their own weapons because UN and NATO peacekeeping forces would protect them. Some 100,000 Bosnians were killed before enough weapons were smuggled to them, in violation of the UN embargo, to make the war more costly for the Serbs. While it is well-understood that a trained army can almost always defeat a far larger group of unorganized civilians, armed civilians can ensure that any attempt at wide-scale slaughter becomes sufficiently costly to serve as a serious deterrent.

WILL THE UN AND THE INTERNATIONAL COMMUNITY PROTECT DISARMED CIVILIANS?

If the UN and the NGOs active in the campaign for a small arms treaty succeed, and people in many nations are disarmed, can the UN and the international community be relied upon to protect those people from government massacres or even genocide? Sadly, the record argues otherwise. United Nations Peacekeepers assured the unarmed people of Rwanda and Srebrenica that they would protect them, then failed to act when the men, women and children gathered in UN designated "safe areas" were massacred. Thousands of Rwandans, disarmed by laws passed in 1964 and 1979, fled to UN troop bases when the genocide began in 1994. Contrary to their promises, the UN troops withdrew, leaving the Rwandan refugees to their fate. The "Independent Inquiry into the Actions of the United Nations During the 1994 Genocide in Rwanda" concluded: "The manner in which troops left, including attempts to pretend to the refugees that they were not, in fact, leaving, was disgraceful."31

The following year, Srebrenica, a UN-designated safe area, was packed with Bosnian Muslim refugees as Bosnian Serb general Radislav Krstic began a week-long rampage there. The Dutch peacekeepers, charged with protecting the refugees, stood aside as the Serbs entered. Not a shot was fired. Krstic and his troops separated 7500 men and boys from the women, drove them off and shot them. A former United Nations commander in Bosnia told a Dutch parliamentary inquiry into the massacre "that it was clear to him that Dutch authorities would not sacrifice its (sic) soldiers for the enclave."32

As I write, black Africans of the Darfur region of Sudan have been under attack for months by Arab militias armed by the Sudanese government. Sudanese Arab nomads have been persecuting black Muslims in the Darfur region for years. Although firearms were difficult to procure, some black self-defense groups had obtained weapons on the black market—illicit weapons—with which they were protecting black farming communities. Then in mid-2003 the Sudanese government began arming the Arab Janjaweed militias. The government bombed the black villages and has been permitting the Arab militias to attack the blacks at will. The United Nations has repeatedly failed to act to protect the Darfur population. Instead, as in Bosnia, it has authorized an arms embargo.33 The BBC News reported that "U.N. Secretary General Kofi Annan refused to use the term genocide [about this situation], which would carry a legal obligation to act."34 While the UN has dithered, 70,000 people have been killed. Thousands of others are threatened with murder and starvation. Although Sudan's gun laws are severe, international small arms control groups argue that these laws are not strict enough. Stricter laws would not prevent the government of Sudan from arming its allies, the Arab militias, while keeping their intended victims defenseless.

Bearing this history in mind, it is easy to understand why many of the world's tyrannical governments would be only too happy to sign the UN firearms protocol and any future global treaty meant to help them disarm their civilians. Samuel Wheeler writes:

**Death and life
in Rwanda
and Bosnia.**

It is hard to see how a United Nations interested in the safety of persons rather than nations could hold that disarming the citizenry is a good idea. In none of the deadly sequence of genocides and citizen-slaughters that have characterized the Third World in the eighties and nineties have ordinary citizens been better off for having been helpless before the assaults of government agents. It is hard to avoid the conclusion that the United Nations initiative is concerned with the interests of nation-states rather than the interests of people. 35

WILL DISARMING CITIZENS REDUCE CRIME?

A fundamental principle of the global arms control campaign is the belief that restricting civilian access to firearms will reduce crime.36 Peaceful citizens could expect to lead safer lives. But since the focus of the arms control agreement is not on removing weapons from criminals and terrorists, but on the far easier task of removing them from the citizenry, it is unlikely that legislation of this sort will succeed. The policy of disarming the public in order to deprive lawless individuals of weapons has been a dramatic failure in Great Britain and other countries where it has been tried. When the British government embarked upon a policy of gun controls in 1920, armed crime was almost non-existent, and violent crime very low.37 In 1904, before Britain had firearms restrictions, there were only four armed robberies in London, then one of the largest cities in the world.38 Seventy years and many gun control laws later, armed robbery in Britain had increased 400 times to 1600 cases.39 The BBC commented that Britain's firearms restrictions "seem to have had little impact on the criminal underworld," but that is not exactly true.40 Disarming law-abiding people has emboldened criminals, who have less to fear from potential victims. From 1989 through 1996, armed crime in England and Wales increased by 500 percent, at the very time that the number of firearms certificate holders decreased by 20 percent.

And in the five years after passage of the sweeping 1997 handgun ban and confiscation of registered handguns, handgun crime had doubled. From 1991 to 1995, crimes against the person in England's inner cities increased 91 percent, and in the four years from 1997 to 2001, the rate of violent crime more than doubled.41 Figures just released for January to September 2004 reported 10,670 firearms offenses recorded by the police, up 500 from the previous year.42 As British rates of violent crime and gun crime have been rising, they have been falling in America, where there are some 200 million privately-owned firearms. The latest surveys by the U.S. Bureau of Justice Statistics found firearms-related crime in America had declined to record levels, while the violent crime rate had fallen 54% since 1993.43

* * *

TIME TO RECONSIDER

Those laboring to enact a global treaty restricting small arms are well-intentioned, but the problem of making the world safer for individuals, rather than for governments, is a more complex matter than merely ratcheting down civilian-owned guns. As Aaron Karp, no opponent of the effort, points out: "unlike other weapons issues, small arms are not primarily about states. More so than almost any other problem of peace and security, small arms direct attention to the rights and practices of individuals."44 Those who believe a more peaceful world can be achieved by restricting private firearms need to consider the basic premises of their campaign—that the public is safer when governments and their agents have a monopoly on firearms. If Oxfam truly intends, as its mission statement claims, "to enable people to exercise their rights and manage their own lives;" if Amnesty International really wants to promote "internationally recognized human rights;" if the United Nations takes seriously the Universal Declaration of Human Rights affirmation that "Everyone has the right to life, liberty and security of person," individual citizens must be permitted the means to defend themselves.45

NOTES

* This article originally appeared in MIT Security Studies Program (SSP0: Breakthroughs, Spring 2005, Volume XIV, No. 1. Reprinted with permission of the author.

1. Alister Doyle, "Action urged on deadly small arms trafficking," Reuters, April 24, 2003. The article refers to small arms as "including machine guns and shoulder fired anti-tank weapons," but according to the UN *Small Arms Survey,* "small arms" do not include anti-tank weapons. They are defined as "revolvers and self-loading pistols, rifles and carbines, assault rifles, sub-machine guns, and light machine guns." "Light weapons" are "heavy machine guns, hand-held grenade launchers, portable anti-tank and anti-aircraft guns, recoilless rifles, portable launchers of anti-tank and anti-aircraft missile systems, and mortars of less than 1-mm caliber." *Small Arms Survey, 2002: Counting the Human Cost*, Graduate Institute of International Studies, Geneva (Oxford, 2002), p. 10. And see UN Report, "General and Complete Disarmament: Small Arms," August, 1997, especially pp. 11-12.

2. These figures are widely cited. See for example, Jayantya Dhanapala, "Multilateral Cooperation on Small Arms and Light Weapons: From Crisis to Collective Response," *The Brown Journal of World Affairs,* Spring 2002, vol. IX, issue 1, p. 163. Dhanapala is the UN Under-Secretary-General for Disarmament Affairs. But these tallies for military deaths from small arms and for civilian deaths are wildly exaggerated as I explain below.

3. On December 24, 2001 the UN General Assembly adopted without vote Resolution 56/24 V on "The illicit trade in small arms and light weapons in all its aspects." Two journals have devoted issues in 2002 to essays on the UN Small Arms Conference held in New York in July 2001. Nearly all the authors are supporters of disarmament. See *The Brown Journal of World Affairs*, Spring 2002, vol. IX, issue 1 and SAIS Review, Winter-Spring, 2002.

4. Some 200 NGOs attended the UN Conference on the Illicit Trade in Small Arms and Light Weapons in All Its Aspects held in New York July 9-20, 2001. On the notion that there is little important distinction between illicit and licit weapons see Nicholas Marsh, "Two Sides of the Same Coin? The Legal and Illegal Trade in Small Arms," *The Brown Journal*, Spring 2002, vol. IX, issue 1, p. 217.

5. *Ibid.*

6. The full title is the Programme of Action to Prevent, Combat, and Eradicate the Illicit Trade in Small Arms and Light Weapons in All Its Aspects.

7. Dhanapala, "Multilateral Cooperation on Small Arms and Light Weapons," p. 168.

8. "Millions of Small Arms in Civilian Hands Pose a Danger to Public Security," *Gambia Daily News,* Banjul, January 10, 2005, posted to the web January 10, 2005.

9. Nairobi Firearms Protocol, International Action Network on Small Arms (IANSA) summary, April 23, 2004.

10. Michael Wines, "In South Africa, Licensing Law Poses Hurdles for Gun Buyers," *The New York Times*, January 3, 2005.

11. *Ibid.* The South African law requires that the police interview three acquaintances of the applicant, each applicant must pass a firearms course, install a safe or strongbox that meets police specifications, and finally have a "good reason" to have a gun. The police refuse to explain what might be a good reason for fear, a firearms specialist explains, that it "would come to be like a template...So they're being very subjective." The backlog of applications is immense with the police agency wrestling with shortages of "items as basic as printed explanations of the law."

12. *Ibid.*

13. "'Face' signature campaign on arms control to be launched," EDS: Updating with Press Conference, Tokyo, December 17, 2004.

14. *Ibid.*

15. The leading role of NGOs Oxfam International and Amnesty International in promoting civilian disarmament would seem to fly in the face of the mission statements of these organizations. Oxfam International, for example, proclaims, "In all our actions Oxfam's goal is to enable people to exercise their rights and manage their own lives." Amnesty International describes itself as "a worldwide movement of people who campaign for internationally recognized human rights." Despite the work of Amnesty International to protect such rights as free speech, it seems it does not recognize self-defense as a legitimate human right.

16. The Japanese government has taken the lead in the push to control small arms. In 1995 it was Japan that introduced Resolution 9 at the UN calling for the international study of small arms laws and use. It has also

sponsored and taken a leading part in the many meetings that have followed. Japan has the strictest gun control of any democracy. Its history with firearms is peculiar, having long banned possession of firearms, swords and other weapons to anyone under the noble class. Weapons were collected from the rest of the population on the pretence that they would be made into a large statute of Buddha. One historian has argued that this policy that deprived the peasants of their weapons reversed the growing social mobility of that class and put it into reverse. The popular attitude toward government and authority is also distinct from that of Americans and Western Europeans. Kopel concludes in his study of Japanese firearms regulation: "More than the people of any other democracy, the Japanese accept the authority of their police and trust their government." See David B. Kopel, *The Samurai the Mountie, and the Cowboy* (Buffalo, New York, 1992), p. 39. For a summary of the Japanese history of firearms regulations see Kopel, pp. 20-58.

17. David B. Kopel, Paul Gallant, Joanne D. Eisen, "Global Deaths from Firearms: Searching for Plausible Estimates," presented to "The Legal, Economic and Human Rights Implications of Civilian Firearms Ownership and Regulation," international symposium, May 1-2, 2003, London.

18. Kopel, Gallant and Eisen, "Global Deaths from Firearms," pp. 3, 11.

19. "At Gunpoint: The Small Arms and Light Weapons Trade: Introduction," *Brown Journal*, Spring 2002, vol. IX, issue 1, p. 159.

20. *Ibid.*, note 1.

21. Kopel et. al., note 1 citing *Small Arms Survey*, p. 65.

22. Mitsuro Donowaki, "Prologue," Report presented to the UN General Assembly, 27 August 1997. And see the articles in *The Brown Journal,* Spring 2002 and SAIS Review, Winter-Spring, 2002 where authors easily switch from the reference to small arms and light weapons (SALW) to small arms alone.

23. Fifty-second Session, Item 71(b) of provisional agenda, United Nations General Assembly.

24. "Suicide and Homicide by People with Mental Illness," *British Medical Journal*, vol. 318, 8 May, 1999, 1225-1226.

25. Kopel, *The Samurai, the Mountie, and the Cowboy*, p. 43. American suicide rates are also lower than European countries with lower rates of gun ownership. See Gary Kleck and Don B. Kates, Armed: New Perspectives on Gun Control (Amherst, New York, 2001), pp. 58-61.

26. See Kopel, Gallant and Eisen, "Global Deaths from Firearms."

27. WHO Small Arms (c. 79,000 deaths annually), compare with the slightly higher figure given by a CDC Report for a different year in the 1990s given in E.G. Krug, et. al., "World Report on Violence and Health," Geneva, 2002).

28. Cited by Don B. Kates in testimony at the UN Human Rights Commission, Geneva, 2003.

29. American opposition to gun registration dates to the Second World War when Americans witnessed the Nazis imposing total firearm bans in countries they invaded and using existing gun registration lists to disarm the people they conquered. John Gleeson, "Recoil from Evil: U.S. Spurned Gun Registration as Hitler's Handy Tool," The Winnipeg Sun, August 20, 2004.

30. Don B. Kates, "Human Rights and Genocide: The Misguided International Public Health Effort to Disarm Civilian Populations," paper presented at the WFSA Symposium, London, May 2, 2003. Also see Don B. Kates, "Democide and Disarmament," *SAIS Review*, vol. XXIII, no. 1 (2003), p. 308.

31. Cited by Dave Kopel, Paul Gallant and Joanne Eisen, "The right to bear arms could have saved Sudan," National Review Online, August 18, 2004.

32. Dave Kopel, Paul Gallant and Joanne Eisen, "When Policy Kills," National Review online, January 27, 2002.

33. Sudan won considerable sympathy at the UN with its insistence that any international action to protect the Darfur blacks would be an unwarranted interference with its national sovereignty.

34. BBC News, June 30, 2004 cited by Kopel, Gallant and Eisen, "The right to bear arms could have saved Sudan."

35. Samuel C. Wheeler, III, "Arms as Insurance," *Public Affairs Quarterly*, vol. XIII, no. 1 (April, 1999), p. 121.

36. See for example Jayantha Dhanapala, "Multilateral Cooperation on Small Arms," p. 163-164.

37. See Joyce L. Malcolm, *Guns and Violence: The English Experience* (Cambridge, Mass., 2002).

38. *Ibid.*, p. 209.

39. *Ibid.*

40. Joyce Lee Malcolm, "Gun Control's Twisted Outcome," *Reason Magazine*, November 2002, p. 22.

41. *Ibid.*

42. BBC News, "Violent crime increases by 6%," BBC News online, January 25, 2005.

43. Jerry Seper, *The Washington Times*, August 17, 2004.

44. Aaron Karp, "The Small Arms Challenge: Back to the Future," *The Brown Review, Spring*, 2002, vol. IX, issue 1, p. 189.

45. See the websites of Oxfam, Amnesty International and the United Nations Universal Declaration of Human Rights.

THE UNITED NATIONS AND THE FUTURE OF HUNTING, SPORT SHOOTING AND FIREARMS OWNERSHIP

BOB BARR

INTRODUCTION

The United Nations was established in the immediate aftermath of World War II amidst great fanfare and towering rhetoric. The mission of this successor to the failed League of Nations was to prevent the "scourge of war," to "reaffirm our faith in fundamental human rights," and establish conditions under which justice . . . and international law can be maintained." While the notion that global disarmament was a part of the organization's mission has been widely presumed since the UN's birth, it

was not until the mid-1990s that UN bureaucrats and anti-firearms NGOs (non-governmental organizations) began the process of including regulation of "small arms and light weapons" in their rhetoric and as a formal component of their self-defined mission.

Now, as we near the end of the first decade of the 21st Century, the fact that the United Nations and its advocates have been declaring for more than a decade that "small arms and light weapons" are a part of their bailiwick, there is coming to be general acceptance of this fact. This has become the case even though there is no basis whatsoever in fact, history, or law to support the notion that the United Nations has any jurisdiction over the ownership, use or transfer of what generally is understood to constitute "small arms and light weapons" (in short, non-military weapons).

Indeed, we are on the verge of witnessing the United Nations draft an international, legally-binding treaty – an Arms Trade Treaty or "ATT" – that likely will purport to regulate not only international aspects of firearms ownership, transfers and markings, but indirectly if not directly, certain domestic aspects of the "right to keep and bear arms." Obviously, this is a dangerous and intolerable situation that must be resisted not only at the United Nations, but in the Congress, the Administration, and even in state capitols across America and in other foreign and international forums.

United Nations Headquarters in New York

HISTORY

This current UN small arms effort had its official inception in 1995 at a UN conference on crime. The end of the Cold War six years earlier left the UN and the "disarmament establishment" (academics and think tanks) with a great deal of time on their hands. They therefore decided that "small arms and light weapons" would be an appropriate "disarmament" issue. As good bureaucrats do, they simply began to discuss and consider the matter as presumed to be within their jurisdiction; unfortunately, they were not stopped early on.

In addition, several individual governments had earlier decided the small arms matter should be on the international agenda. Japan was the leader of this group. This was facilitated because of the fact that, unfortunately, firearms within the United States had become a domestic issue in Japan in 1992. That year, a Japanese exchange student, Yoshihiro Hattori, was accidentally killed in New Orleans by a firearm. This story motivated the Japanese to pursue the issue in the international arena. Then, in 1997 the Land Mine Treaty was adopted and this motivated NGOs to attempt to do the same thing with small arms. The situation was further exacerbated by tragic incidents such as the 1999 Columbine shooting, which received widespread media coverage around the world.

Between 1995 and 2001 two parallel UN processes on small arms developed. The first was an effort to draft a crime-oriented "Firearms Protocol," or treaty, by the UN Crime Prevention Branch in Vienna, Austria. The other was a disarmament-based effort to control small arms throughout the world by a global treaty or some other disarmament regime.

The effort in support of a crime-oriented "Firearms Protocol" was part of a larger endeavor to draft a convention against "Transnational Organized Crime (TOC)." (Note: A "convention" is a treaty which has multiple countries as parties.) Both the TOC and the Firearms Protocol were adopted by the UN in 2001. The Firearms Protocol has not been adopted by the United States, but has gained credibility because it is in effect in the European Union and a number of other countries. The Protocol's most significant provision concerns the marking of firearms with individual serial numbers. It requires the marking of all firearms with unique serial numbers -- except for those manufactured in China (the country where large quantities of automatic weapons used by rogue regimes are manufactured)! In the Firearms Protocol drafting process, China successfully insisted on a special exception to the requirement as its price for supporting the Protocol. In addition, state-to-state transfers for security reasons were also exempted from marking requirement. The Firearms Protocol began a pattern which still exists today for this entire series of international "small arms" efforts – member states cleverly ma-

"Non Violence" - This sculpture was a gift from the Government of Luxembourg presented to the United Nations in 1988. It consists of a large replica in bronze of a 45-calibre revolver, the barrel of which is tied into a knot. It was created in 1980 as a peace symbol by artist Karl Fredrik Reutersward, and is located in the Visitor's Plaza, facing First Avenue at 45th Street.

nipulating the processes and ensuring the provisions apply only to industries or civilians in selected states.

An even more important push on the international small arms issue arose from activities of the UN Department for Disarmament Affairs during the years 1995 to 2001. It was during this period that two UN experts groups laid the foundation for the attempt at a global treaty or a UN disarmament regime covering small arms. The irony of this effort was that it was a "disarmament" initiative aimed not at nation states but at civilians. It is commonly accepted knowledge today that of the approximately 700 million firearms in the world, some 70% are legally held by civilians. Two reports were published that, among other things, defined what "small arms" were and called for a major international conference on the subject.

Problematically, "small arms and light weapons" ("small arms" for short) are routinely defined by the United Nations and its component entities and related endeavors in the broadest possible terms, to include virtually all rifles, pistols and revolvers (and probably shotguns if considered "hunting firearms"). Homemade firearms were also included. Despite efforts by the United States to properly limit "small arms and light weapons" to include only military-type, automatic weapons, the UN continues to operate and to further its anti-firearms agenda based on definitions of firearms that include virtually all military and civilian firearms.

As noted, the reports recommended a major international conference in 2001 to consider the issue. The conference did occur and we are living with the result of that meeting even today.

Numerous preparatory meeting were held prior to the 2001 small arms and light weapons conference, during which time it became clear there were major divisions between the United States and many other countries that were already, or were planning to be, active in the process. Among other contentious issues which emerged was whether the conference would make any recommendation regarding -- or even reference to -- civilian firearms ownership. Anti-gun NGOs (the international version of domestic gun control groups), such as the ever-present and well-funded IANSA (International Action Network on Small Arms), viewed the conference as an opportunity to further a radical gun control agenda, especially if they could somehow move the gathering in the direction of producing a treaty – or at least start the process for a treaty – limiting or severely regulating civilian ownership.

The 2001 conference used a "consensus" decision-making process whereby one country (usually a major country) could block any one particular provision of the conference report. This is where the United States affirmatively exerted itself. John Bolton, at the time the US Under Secretary of State with responsibility for disarmament matters, delivered a forceful speech the very first day of the conference. In his address, which truly shocked many of the delegates because of its frankness and forcefulness (I know; I was there as an official, "private sector advisor" to the U.S. delegation), Bolton clearly explained the problem from America's perspective, and he laid down certain US "red lines" that would not be crossed. He told the gathering:

> "Excellencies and distinguished colleagues, it is my honor and privilege to present United States views at this United Nations Conference on the Illicit Trade in Small Arms and Light Weapons in All its Aspects.
>
> The abstract goals and objectives of this Conference are laudable. Attacking the global illicit trade in small arms and light weapons (SA/LW) is an important initiative which the international community should, indeed must, address because of its wide ranging effects. The illicit trade in SA/LW can be used to exacerbate conflict, threaten

civilian populations in regions of conflict, endanger the work of peacekeeping forces and humanitarian aid workers, and greatly complicate the hard work of economically and politically rebuilding war-torn societies. Alleviating these problems is in all of our interest.

Small arms and light weapons, in our understanding, are the strictly military arms -- automatic rifles, machine guns, shoulder-fired missile and rocket systems, light mortars -- that are contributing to continued violence and suffering in regions of conflict around the world. **We separate these military arms from firearms such as hunting rifles and pistols, which are commonly owned and used by citizens in many countries. As U.S. Attorney General John Ashcroft has said, "just as the First and Fourth Amendments secure individual rights of speech and security respectively, the Second Amendment protects an individual right to keep and bear arms." The United States believes that the responsible use of firearms is a legitimate aspect of national life.** Like many countries, the United States has a cultural tradition of hunting and sport shooting. We, therefore, do not begin with the presumption that all small arms and light weapons are the same or that they are all problematic. It is the illicit trade in military small arms and light weapons that we are gathered here to address and that...

We do not support measures that would constrain legal trade and legal manufacturing of small arms and light weapons..." (emphasis added)

Eventually the conference did adopt what it called a "Programme of Action" or "POA" on small arms. Though it purported not to address civilian firearms possession, by virtue of its broad definitional base and the potential scope of its proposals that inevitably would impact domestic regulations, the POA presented a clear threat to domestic ownership of civilian firearms. The Second Amendment was in danger of being limited by an international process!

The POA event began an ambitious series of projects calling for countries to examine brokering, general regulation of small arms and other matters. The "Programme" also called for "Biennial Meetings of States" (BMS) to strengthen its claim to legitimacy and to keep the issues with which it purported to deal alive until receptive administrations took office in non-supportive countries (in other words, the United States). These proposed meetings would continue discussion on the POA and seek further international action.

In fact, despite US opposition, biennial meetings were held in 2003 and 2005; and a final, "Review Conference" was convened in 2006. The 2006 meeting was to be the launching pad for yet another multi-year series of meetings to further the ambitious, anti-firearms agenda laid out five years before at the 2001 meeting. At all these meeting the same issues seemed to emerge and the same players seemed to take the same sides. The US continued to defend civilian firearms ownership and argue against its inclusion in the deliberations; it also continued to resist efforts at promulgating a comprehensive international treaty on small arms. In addition, the US took the position that no further work was needed on the POA, and that continued series of conferences and meetings served no legitimate purpose.

By this time – in 2006 – John Bolton had become the acting US Ambassador to the United Nations; and his prior position as Under Secretary of State was filled by Bob Joseph, who shared Bolton's commitment to ensuring the United Nations did not gain a foothold over our constitutionally-guaranteed right to keep and bear arms. Their leadership in this effort caused the 2006 Review Conference to end in stalemate without a report. Unfortunately, as with other UN efforts, failure is viewed as temporary only, and the organization simply continued its anti-firearms agenda in other forums.

After the failure of the 2006 Review Conference, most of the "action" on small arms shifted to the UN General Assembly. In October 2006, for example, proponents of international firearms regulation were successful in a series of initiatives, including the launching of the ATT process, beginning an effort on arms brokering, and commencing a move on ammunition regulation. And – of course -- another BMS was authorized for 2008.

MARKING AND TRACING – BROKERING – AMMUNITION

In 1995 a UN group, after extensive meetings and negotiations, put forward an "instrument" on marking and tracing of firearms. This was not a treaty, to which the US again objected, but a political "arrangement" between states. The instrument followed the earlier UN Firearms Protocol requiring the marking of all firearms, but again contained an exception for China. The agreement also called for cooperation between police departments, including INTERPOL and other international and multi-national agencies.

In 1997 a similar group produced an instrument on "arms brokering," calling counties to enact legislation and to cooperate in fighting illegal arms brokering. Like so many UN documents, it failed to properly or reasonably define what constituted "arms brokering" because agreement could not be reached between the parties.

The UN now is in the process of considering what it calls "Problems Arising From the Accumulation of Conventional Ammunition Stockpiles in Surplus." This effort is scheduled to produce a report for the October 2008 session of the General Assembly. For some reason, in this particular process, ammunition and the regulation of ammunition have been of particular concern to Germany. Initial proposals were extremely ambitious in calling for record keeping and tracing of ammunition based on box lot number, and even a requirement that individual lot numbers be included in each cartridge's head stamp! The ammunition industry understandably was and remains very concerned about these proposals, which are extremely impractical and costly; billions upon billions of rounds of ammunition are produced each year, and any attempt at record keeping would be doomed to failure.

The above descriptions of UN efforts to regulate, limit and control firearms are extremely cursory and mere summaries of events and issues. They describe but the tip of the anti-firearms iceberg that constitutes the UN agenda in this arena. Each meeting or event involves weeks of meeting, reams of papers, consultations, and lobbying on behalf of governments and NGOs alike.

THE ARMS TRADE TREATY EFFORT

Of all the international initiatives aimed at small arms, none is more serious than that of the on-going push for an Arms Trade Treaty. The principal proponent of an ATT has been the government of the UK. An ATT would supposedly control and prevent the transfer of arms to governments which abuse human rights, criminals and non-state actors, such as rebel groups. Successive UK governments have been criticized for allowing arms deals to human rights abusers. The government of Prime Minister Tony Blair also took a significant amount of heat for its support of the US war in Iraq. Oddly enough, the UK defense industry supports an ATT as a means to make import/export criteria uniform throughout the world. It is much easier to export your goods when you only have one set of regulations to deal with; and at the same time and by the same token, it is much easier for such activities to be monitored and controlled by an international "authority" if there is a single, uniform set of procedures required. The resolution that began the multi-year ATT process passed in 2006 by a vote of 153 to 1. The United States, with John Bolton still then serving as our country's UN Ambassador, cast the US the sole negative vote.

At this time there are no definitive drafts of a future Arms Trade Treaty. To be sure, however, the process continues apace. Throughout 2008 a "Group of Government Experts" ("GGE") will meet on the feasibility and the scope of a possible ATT. The group will make a report to the October 2008 UN General Assembly, which probably will pass another resolution establishing an "Open Ended Working Group" to draft the actual instrument. This group would likely then meet in 2010, following a series of workshops and meetings in 2009 to cultivate support for an ATT. The final product can be expected thereafter.

Another aspect of this which cannot be ignored is the impression (actually, the illusion) it offers the world that "disarmament" is being furthered. The UN has been singularly unsuccessful at controlling nuclear proliferation (and most everything else it has attempted), but it can point to the small arms effort and claim some sort of "success," if for no reason other than the process remains alive and well within its massive bureaucracies. The reality is that many states have exempted themselves from any real provisions of what may have been adopted. More problematically, the process masks the true, anti-firearms (and anti-US) agenda of many of its member nations (and many officials at the UN itself).

Anti-gun groups have adopted the ATT as their great hope. There are several reasons for this, not the least of which is that once the treaty process has started it is hard to stop. All the countries and diplomats involved have a vested interest in seeing the process conclude successfully. Once the ATT treaty process begins in earnest, there will be an ATT. If there comes a time in which the Congress remains in control of leaders sympathetic to the UN agenda, and if the White House were similarly occupied, the entire treaty process could be accelerated in order to take advantage of such a "favorable" scenario.

There are, of course, unique aspects of United States treaty law that must be kept in mind when evaluating the dangers of an ATT. First, if a treaty is ratified by the US Senate it becomes domestic US law, on par with other laws actually passed by the Congress and signed by a president. Second, unless affirmatively rejected by the Senate pursuant to a recorded vote, treaties "hang around" forever, and can be brought to a vote if the winds become favorable, at any time (perhaps years after initially presented). The politics of the US, as the politics of any body, shift over time from left to right and back again. Given the right circumstances and right number of votes, a very radical anti-gun ATT could be adopted by the Senate and become law in US with very little, if any, public awareness or input.

An ATT could do any or all of several things. It might ban civilian possession of "military firearms" (very broadly defined as so-called "assault weapons"); it might require universal registration of firearms; and it very well might mandate the licensing, registering and proof-of-need for all civilian firearms owners. Such a treaty also could essentially prohibit the civilian transport of firearms across national borders (for hunting or shooting competition) without an export license and a fee being paid. Other, more radical suggestions in the UN process include age limits, bans on handguns, requirements that guns are kept at police stations, and that hunters are allowed only one-shot weapons with a range of 100 yards.

CONCLUSION

There is real danger that throughout these processes the participants will adopt carte blanche some or all of the more radical proposals mentioned above. What is equally problematic, however, is that the steps its proponents might take will inadvertently impact legitimate collectors, hunters and sport shooters' interests without ever being made aware of those interests. Most diplomats and UN bureaucrats have never held a firearm, have never been hunting, or target shooting. They are constantly bombarded with anti-gun propaganda from well-funded anti-gun NGOs, led by IANSA. Moreover, the countries from which many of these officials hail have neither the firearms history nor the constitutionally-recognized, fundamental "human right" to possess firearms for legitimate purposes, including self-defense. Many of these officials are disdainful that we in the United States do recognize and enjoy such a right.

Countering this concerted and long-term (actually, never-ending) effort by the United Nations and most of its member states requires a multi-pronged offensive: proactive and consistent political effort in the US at all levels of government; support for the firearms industry and firearms retailers; and supporting hunting and shooting organizations that have taken the initiative to become engaged and involved at the UN. The bottom line is, we must consciously educate our fellow citizens as to the importance of the Second Amendment and of our nation's sovereignty, and alert them and our political leaders as to the insidious and destructive nature of what the United Nations is up to in this regard. Failure to take all these steps could result in catastrophic damage to our right to keep and bear arms.

CONTRIBUTORS

JEANINE BAKER has a PhD in Natural Resources and Agriculture. Her background is in popula-tion dynamics, with a focus on the effect of non-native species on the economy, the environment and social values of a region. Risk assessments to resolve complex problems with stakeholder conflicts and computer simulations form a major part of her work. She has a strong academic interest in the issues surrounding legal versus illegal firearms ownership, legislation and violent crime. This interest has led to research into trends for suicide and violent crime with firearms and the search for underlying causes resulting in changes to these trends.

MARK BARNES has a private law practice in Washington, D.C., His clients include variety of do-mestic and international businesses, institutional organizations and private individuals. Mr. Barnes spe-cializes in representing clients with regulatory and legislative interests requiring attention before the Congress and federal government agencies. He also represents clients with sensitive and complex policy matters necessitating the formulation and oversight of domestic and foreign initiatives. He is the spokesperson for FAIR Trade Group, an organization of businesses involved in the legal import and export of firearms across international borders Mr. Barnes received his law degree from the UCLA School of Law in 1981 and his Bachelor of Science Degree in Political Science from Arizona State University in 1978 where he graduated summa cum laude and a member of Phi Beta Kappa.

BOB BARR represented the 7th District of Georgia in the U. S. House of Representatives from 1995 to 2003. He now occupies the 21st Century Liberties Chair for Freedom and Privacy at the American Conservative Union. Bob also serves as a Board Member of the National Rifle Association. Bob Barr heads a consulting firm, Liberty Strategies LLC, headquartered in Atlanta, Georgia, and with an office in the Washington, DC area. He writes and speaks widely on civil liberties, especially the right to pri-vacy. In fact, recognizing Bob Barr's leadership in privacy matters, *New York Times* columnist William Safire has called him "Mr. Privacy."

FEDERATION OF ASSOCIATION FOR HUNTING AND CONSERVATION OF THE EU (FACE) is an international, non-profit making, non-governmental organization that represents its 36 Full Members that are the national hunters' associations within the Member States of the European Union and other Council of Europe countries, as well as its four Associate Members. From its head-quarters in the heart of Brussels, Belgium, FACE has acted in the interests of over 7 million European hunters since 1977. FACE seeks to: PROMOTE hunting as a tool for rural development, for conser-vation of wildlife and biodiversity, and for the conservation, improvement and restoration of wildlife habitats; ADVOCATE the collective interests of its members at the level of European and international institutions in order that the interests of hunters are taken into account in relation to hunting, wildlife the Marketing Department of Norma. Presently advertisements, product information, fairs, writing for the personnel magazines, translations, presentations, and hunting projects occupy her time. Becoming a hunter five years ago, she has found this to be a great source of inspiration, and she is always ready to learn something new in this field.

CHRISTER HOLMGREN, born in 1942, is a gunsmith, writer and journalist. With forty years of professional gunsmithing behind him, he has both breadth and depth of knowledge about firearms and ammunition. This knowledge and his enthusiasm and interest as a hunter, have made him a well-respected author of editorial texts on hunting and firearms in the Swedish hunting press, as well as two larger books, "The Firearm and the Hunt" and "Shooting in Practice." A third book with the working title "Rifle Hunting" is also under production. Besides conventional hunting, He has a great interest in experimental archeology and hunting with prehistoric bows. He is one of few hunters in the world who is capable of making his own bi-faced flint arrow heads, arrows and replicas of prehistoric longbows and with that equipment has successfully brought down a number of medium-sized game during his hunts in Africa.

JOYCE LEE MALCOLM is an historian and professor at George Mason University School of Law and fellow of the Royal Historical Society. She specializes in the fields of common law, constitutional history and war and law. She is the author of seven books, including TO KEEP AND BEAR ARMS: THE ORIGINS OF AN ANGLO-AMERICAN RIGHT and GUNS AND VIOLENCE: THE ENGLISH EXPERIENCE, both published by Harvard University Press as well as numerous articles published in legal and historical journals.

GARY MAUSER is a professor emeritus in the Institute for Canadian Urban Research Studies, Faculty of Business Administration, Simon Fraser University, Canada. Recent publications include, "Would Banning Firearms Reduce Murder and Suicide? A Review of International Evidence," Harvard Journal of Law and Public Policy, (co-author Don B. Kates) 2007. He has made invited presentations to the United Nations Conference on Small Arms and Light Weapons, the Canadian Senate and the House of Commons, and he has testified as an expert witness before the Supreme Court of Canada. For more information please see his website, www.garymauser.net/

SAMARA MCPHEDRAN has a PhD in Psychology from the University of Sydney. She has been researching violent crime for many years, with a strong interest in investigating the causes of violence in intimate partner relationships and community crime. As such, she has researched the effect of firearms legislation; gun policy; gun control and gun laws; Australian and international firearms regulation; firearms and violence. Samara also runs a Statistical and Psychometric Consultancy and has a long time interest in promoting unbiased research and the use of evidence based policy to formulate legislation.

DAVID PENN was employed as Keeper of the Department of Exhibits & Firearms at the Imperial War Museum in London from 1976 until 2005. He was a member, and latterly Chairman, of the Firearms Consultative Committee (a statutory body set up to advise the Home Secretary, throughout its life from 1989 to 2004), has previously served as Hon. Secretary of the Historical Breechloading Smallarms Association, Chairman of the Museums Weapons Group and as a member of various Home Office working groups on firearms related matters. He is currently the Secretary of the British Shooting Sports Council, President of the Arms & Armour Society, the British Association for Shooting and management, nature conservation, firearms, animal health, game meat, and so forth; CONTRIBUTE towards informing decision-makers, media and the public at large as to two principles of sustainable hunting and biodiversity conservation, by raising awareness to initiatives that aim to promote these principles and the management of the wise and sustainable use of natural resources.

FRANZ CSÁSZÁR was born in Vienna, Austria in 1940. He holds a Doctor of Laws degree (1964) from the University of Vienna. He was a member of Institute of Criminal Law and Criminology, Law Faculty, University of Vienna from 1964 to 2003 and a Professor of Criminology and Criminalistics from 1983 to 2003. His main fields of research are: development of crime, juvenile delinquency; regional sentencing disparities; interrelations between crime and social reactions. He was a Sworn Court Expert from 1973 to 2003, specializing in handwriting and questioned documents, tool marks, and crime reconstruction. He is a Lecturer at Police Academy. Since 1997, he has been president of "IWÖ – Interessengemeinschaft Liberales Waffenrecht in Österreich", a non-profit organisation dedicated to keeping Austria's traditional firearms laws.

ALAN GOTTLIEB is a Nuclear Engineering graduate of the University of Tennessee and attended the Institute on Comparative Political & Economic Systems at Georgetown University. Alan is the Chairman of the Citizens Committee for the Right to Keep and Bear Arms, Founder of the Second Amendment Foundation, a National Director of the American Conservative Union, President of the Center for the Defense of Free Enterprise and President of the American Political Action Committee. Alan is the author of nine books and coauthor of seven others.

JULIANNE VERSNEL GOTTLIEB is the Publisher of the Journal on Firearms & Public Policy. She is also the Publisher of Women & Guns magazine, a contributor to Gun Week and Managing Editor of both Point Blank and The Second Amendment Reporter.

JOE GREEN joined New Zealand Police as a constable in 1983 and worked both city and rural areas. As an NCO he coordinated youth education services at the regional level. As inspector Joe has commanded an operational response section, managed a recruiting project, community relations, youth services, arms control, Image Management and vetting services. Prior to joining the police Joe was a primary school teacher, teaching children aged 8 to 13 years. Joe is married to Anne, a kindergarten teacher. They have three adult children and two grandsons. They recently became caregivers and guardians to their 13 year old niece.

COLIN GREENWOOD spent five years in the Coldstream Guards, and then joined the West Yorkshire Police, retiring as a Superintendent after twenty five years. He then became a freelance writer, worked as a forensic firearms examiner and was consultant to a number of organizations. In 1970 he was awarded a Research Fellowship at the Cambridge University Institute of Criminology to research the relationship between gun laws and crime. His book "Firearms Control" (Routledge & Kegan Paul, London) was published in 1972. He has continued to work in this field and has written extensively.

CARIN HÖGLUND, born in 1971, has a background in international marketing and studied in the US and France. She has worked for Norma Precision since 2003. Earlier employments have included assignments within information, international contacts, and sales which have been useful in her work at

Conservation, the Historical Breechloading Smallarms Association and the Muzzle Loaders Association of Great Britain and is a member of the Home Office's Historic Firearms Reference Panel. In 2007 he was appointed advisor to the FESAC Board.

STEPHEN A. PETRONI has been collecting arms & militaria since 1973. He is President of Association of Maltese Arms Collectors & Shooters. He set up historical re-enactment and helped launch target shooting (with muzzle-loaders). From 1991 Stephen directed the discussions with Government aimed at replacing Malta's Colonial-era arms ordinance drafting proposals and sat on a Committee entrusted with proposing the revision of Police policy on the use of arms for collection and target shooting purposes (the Committee's proposals were endorsed by the Cabinet of Ministers on 12 September 1995). Between 2002 and 2005 he successfully negotiated the terms of the draft legislation which became law in July 2005 (Arms Act 2005) and the Arms Licensing Regulations which came into effect along with the Act on 15th August 2006. Stephen was appointed member of the Weapons Board thereafter. In May 2006 he was accepted as a FESAC Board Member representing Malta, also joining the Juridical Committee as a result of which he was involved in the negotiations with the EU institutions over the Arms Directive amendments. Stephen was appointed Chairman of FESAC in 2006 and represents it on the Committee of the European Sports Shooting Forum (ESSF).

The **SPORTING SHOOTERS' ASSOCIATION OF AUSTRALIA** (SSAA) is the legitimate, democratic and peak shooting body in Australia, representing 120,000 recreational rifle, shotgun and pistol sports shooters and hunting members. SSAA National has NGO status at the United Nations and has been an invited guest to many international meetings and conferences. The SSAA Media & Publications team comprises of individuals with qualifications as diverse as Communications, Politics, History and International Security. Together, the SSAA National Representatives work towards creating a better environment and community understanding of all forms of hunting and sports shooting in Australia.

MARY ZEISS STANGE received a B.A. in English Literature from Syracuse University graduating Pi Beta Kappa, with subsequent masters and doctoral degrees in Religion and Culture Studies. She has been an associate professor of women's studies and religion at Skidmore College, where for eight years she served as director of the Women's Studies Program The author of Woman the Hunter (1997), Stange divides her time between teaching in upstate New York and ranching in Montana.

CAROL K. OYSTER received a degree in Psychology from UCLA, a master's in Counseling Psychology from Loyola-Marymount University and a masters and doctorate in Social Psychology from University of Delaware. She is a Professor of Psychology and Women's Studies at University of Wisconsin at La Crosse.

DAVE WORKMAN is an award-winning editor, author and nationally recognized firearms authority. The senior editor of *Gun Week* since November 2000, he is also a contributing editor to *Women & Guns*, and his work also appears frequently in various firearms periodicals including *Gun Digest* and *Gun World*. A native of the Pacific Northwest, Workman grew up in Tacoma, Washington and graduated with a degree in editorial journalism from the University of Washington. A past associate member of the American Society for Law Enforcement Training, Workman spent nine years on the board of directors of the National Rifle Association. He is a certified firearms instructor.